PELICAN BOOKS

DRAMA IN PERFORMANCE

Raymond Williams was born in 1921 at the Welsh border village of Pandy where his father was a railway signalman. He was educated at the village school, at Abergavenny Grammar School, and at Trinity College, Cambridge. After the war, in which he served as an anti-tank captain in the Guards Armoured Division, he became an adult education tutor in the Oxford University Delegacy for Extra-Mural Studies until 1961, when he was elected Fellow of Jesus College, Cambridge, where he is a university Reader in Drama. In 1947 he was an editor of *Politics and Letters*, and later General Editor of the *New Thinker's Library*. He has published a number of essays in literary journals and is well known as a book-reviewer for the *Guardian*. His books include *Drama from Ibsen to Eliot* (1952), *Drama in Performance* (1954), *Culture and Society 1780–1950*, *The Long Revolution* (1961), *Communications* (1962) (all in Penguins), *Modern Tragedy* (1965) and two novels, *Border Country* (in Penguins) and *Second Generation*. Raymond Williams is married and has three children.

D0249686

RAYMOND WILLIAMS

# Drama in Performance

PENGUIN BOOKS

Penguin Books Ltd, Harmondsworth, Middlesex, England
Penguin Books Inc., 7110 Ambassador Road, Baltimore, Maryland 21207, U.S.A.
Penguin Books Australia Ltd, Ringwood, Victoria, Australia

—

First published by Frederick Muller 1954
Revised and extended edition published by C. A. Watts 1968
Published in Pelican Books 1972

—

Copyright © Raymond Williams, 1968

—

Made and printed in Great Britain by
Hazell Watson & Viney Ltd,
Aylesbury, Bucks
Set in Monotype Bembo

This book is sold subject to the condition
that it shall not, by way of trade or otherwise,
be lent, re-sold, hired out, or otherwise circulated
without the publisher's prior consent in any form of
binding or cover other than that in which it is
published and without a similar condition
including this condition being imposed
on the subsequent purchaser

# Contents

# Preface

THIS is a revised and extended version of a book first published by Frederick Muller Ltd in 1954. It contains new chapters on 'plays in transition' – from the Restoration to the Victorian theatre – on modern experimental drama – Eliot, Brecht and Beckett – and on film. The chapters from the earlier book – on *Antigone*, English medieval drama, *Antony and Cleopatra* and *The Seagull* – have been revised, and the concluding argument has been recast.

The original *Drama in Performance* was written after *Drama from Ibsen to Eliot* and in the same year as my essay in *Preface to Film*. I would like this revised book to be read alongside my later work on drama, in *Modern Tragedy* and *Drama from Ibsen to Brecht*. In their present form, these three books were conceived as interrelated.

I wish to thank Mr T. M. Schuller for his help in getting the book out again; Mr Paddy Whannel, of the British Film Institute, for his help in arranging a special showing of a sequence of *Wild Strawberries*; and Mr Göran Printz-Påhlson for help on a point in the Bergman text.

R. W.

# Acknowledgements

THE following acknowledgements are due for the use of copyright material: to W. Judeich, *Topographie von Athen* (Beck), for Fig. 1; to the Clarendon Press and A. Pickard-Cambridge, *The Theatre of Dionysus at Athens*, for Fig. 2; to the Bibliotheek Rijksuniversiteit te Utrecht, for Fig. 3; to All Souls College, Oxford, for Fig. 4; to Dennis Dobson Ltd, *The Seagull Produced by Stanislavsky*, for the basis of Fig. 5; to the Bibliothèque de l'Arsenal, Paris, for Plate 2; to the Musée Condé, Chantilly, and Mr Richard Southern and Faber & Faber Ltd, *Medieval Theatre in the Round*, for Plate 3; to Éditions S.L., Lyon, for Plate 4; to Fotoclere, Turin, for Plate 5; to the Richard Southern Theatre Collection and the University of Bristol for Plates 6 and 7; to Janus Films, New York, for Plates 8–11; to Scott and Wilkinson and Mr Norman Marshall and John Lehmann, *The Other Theatre*, for Plate 12; to J. K. Tyl Theatre, Plzen, and the International Theatre Institute and UNESCO, for Plate 13; to Elizabeth Wyckoff and David Grene and Richard Lattimore, *Greek Tragedies*, Phoenix Books, University of Chicago Press, for translated extracts from *Antigone*; to William Heinemann Ltd, *Works of Henrik Ibsen*, Vol. 1, for translated quotations from *The Feast at Solhoug*; to Faber & Faber Ltd for quotations from T. S. Eliot, *The Family Reunion* and *Poetry and Drama*, and Samuel Beckett, *Waiting for Godot*; to Hartsdale House, New York, for translated quotations from Chekhov, *Plays*; to Dennis Dobson Ltd for quotations from *The Seagull Produced by Stanislavsky*; to Desmond F. Vesey, and Methuen, Bertolt Brecht, *Plays*, for translated extracts from *The Life of Galileo*; to Ingmar Bergman, and to the translators, Lars Malmstrom and David Kushner, *Four Screenplays of Ingmar Bergman*, Martin Secker & Warburg Ltd.

# List of Illustrations

## FIGURES

## PLATES

# 1

# Introduction

THIS book is, in form, a critical essay. Its theme is *drama in performance*, and this appears in three ways: first, in the development of a method of dramatic analysis; second, in an account of the performance of certain selected plays; and, third, in the argument of certain general ideas in the relations between text and performance in drama, and of the consequences of these ideas in dramatic theory.

On each point the treatment is that of an essay, rather than of a systematic work, and this is so not only because the approach is exploratory, in a field in which, as yet, little systematic work has been done, but also because the whole point of my inquiry is historical comparison and movement, which alone, it seems to me, offers a chance of getting beyond some important contemporary assumptions and habits of thought. It would have been impossible even to begin this kind of analysis of, say, a Greek dramatic performance, a medieval religious play, or an Elizabethan or Restoration production, except on the basis of the work (in many cases the life's work) of a number of scholars who have investigated the essential facts. My debts to such work are obvious, and are gratefully acknowledged. But to try to bring the results of that work into play, by comparison and analysis, and to go on to relate them to contemporary dramatic methods and problems, ruled out, from the beginning, any attempt at completeness or at systematic treatment. My questions had begun from my own work on modern drama, and I wanted to be able to range freely, in historical comparisons, in a way that was only possible in an essay.

The questions I am trying to answer can branch in a number of ways, but at root they are one question: what, historically, is the relation between a dramatic text and a dramatic performance? This, I believe, is the fundamental question in dramatic theory, but the only ways of answering it are, in the first instance, practical. I propose to consider a number of plays, drawn from widely separated periods of time, and to examine, in each case, the relation between text and performance. This requires, evidently, a necessary minimum of exposition of the conditions of performance which existed at the time that the play was written. This summary exposition is, in itself, useful, in so far as it allows us to see the historical variety of conditions of performance; for we all, very naturally, tend to construct our idea of performance from our own contemporary experience of it, and this, since it is bound to be limited, may at times be disabling: making us approach a continuing and varied art as if it were a fixed and single habit. But to know the general conditions of performance alone is insufficient; we need to know also, in such detail as we may, the practice which these conditions made possible: the performance as actuality, and not as a generalized account. After stating, therefore, in a general way, the general conditions of performance, I try, in each case, to show how the particular play I have chosen would actually have been performed, choosing, for emphasis, certain particular scenes, which can be considered in reasonable detail.

In every case, a full account of the conditions of performance would require a separate and substantial work. I have tried, instead, to emphasize the dominant features, as being sufficient for my intention; but the reader will realize, not only that for a fuller account he should go to the works which I list at the end, but also that in my summary I have had to make choices, on points on which there is still, among qualified students, considerable disagreement; and that, although I have done this after studying all the evidence and arguments that were available to me, my accounts are still choices, and not verdicts, and are not intended as a substitute for study of the original authorities in these fields. Similarly, where I have given accounts of texts, I have done so as a means to the analysis of the text in performance, and not, obviously, as a complete and self-sufficient study. My accounts, both of general conditions and of texts, are, as I have said, only means to the subsequent analysis of the work in performance, which is my major emphasis. The reader will also be aware, of course, that the analyses of the works chosen are not intended to amount to an account of *all* drama in performance, or even of all its major aspects. I have chosen those aspects which seemed most relevant and interesting; and the plays I have taken are all, I think, representative of major forms. But there are, obviously, many forms which I have not examined; and even within the forms chosen there is often greater variety than I have been able to illustrate. That selection was necessary is obvious; but the actual selection rests, finally, on my own judgement of the major elements in the dramatic tradition which it is now most necessary for us to know and understand.

The method of analysis of each chosen work in performance requires explanation. We can study a written play, and state a response to it, and that statement is, or is intended to be, literary criticism. Alternatively, we can study an actual performance of a play, and state a response to that; and that statement is, or is intended to be, theatrical criticism. For legitimate purposes of emphasis, the study of a text may fail to include any detailed consideration of the way in which that text would be performed, as the author intended it should be performed. Similarly, the study of a performance may isolate the details of performance alone, without particular consideration of the play. These methods have their uses, but, ultimately, dramatic criticism must proceed beyond them. It is an advance to have a literary account of a play, followed by a consideration of its performance; or a theatrical account of a performance, preceded by an account of the play that is being performed. Of these, as of the earlier methods, we have some good examples in the English tradition. But, strangely, we have very few examples of the necessary next stage: a consideration of play and performance, literary text and theatrical representation, not as separate entities, but as the unity which they are intended to become. A casual look may suggest that this procedure is common; but it will be seen, I think, on closer examination, that the literary study and the theatrical are, almost always, in separate compartments. And this is so, I suggest, because of a confusion, both theoretical and practical, in our contemporary understanding of the relation between a dramatic text and a dramatic performance. This relation, it will be remembered, is the main theoretical problem which I am attempting to solve.

My conclusion, however, is not intended to rest solely on formal argument. I have tried, in my analyses of works in performance, to find a method which would be adequate for dramatic criticism, in the full sense in which I have defined it. What I am concerned with is *the written work in performance*: that is to say, the dramatic structure of a work, which we may realize when we read it as literature, as this actually appears when the play is performed. The relation between text and performance will be seen, in practice, to vary; but to bring them together, in analysis, seems to me a necessary emphasis. In much contemporary thinking, a separation between literature and theatre is constantly assumed; yet the drama is, or can be, both literature and theatre, not the one at the expense of the other, but each *because* of the other. It is because I think the separation is now deeply disabling for the drama that I am examining, as a formal point of theory, the relation between text and performance. But this can be treated also, in a more immediate way, by the analysis of the text and performance of actual scenes. I have to depend, of course, in such analysis, on the deliberate exercise of imagination. I cannot recapture the actual performances; but, by approaching each scene from a number of aspects, hope to reconstruct the essential unity. The reader will realize that there can be no documentary certainty of detail; and that imagination can be translated, and derogated, as 'speculation'. But while my attempts will often contain faults, and while I shall be glad to be offered corrections and alternatives, I would claim that the method itself is valid, and necessary. The controls are the known general facts of performance and the existing texts; and it is in this context that my particular exercises of dramatic imagination can be followed and checked. The imaginative effort itself does not need apology. It may, in particular cases, succeed or fail, but it is a faculty which no living study of the art of drama can do without. And I have tried to carry this imaginative emphasis through to what I say, in my concluding arguments, about contemporary dramatic possibilities, and especially about our new means of writing and performance.

I begin where known drama began: in Athens in the fifth century B.C. I take as my example the *Antigone* of Sophocles. I go on to look briefly at some different kinds of English medieval drama, before the building of our first theatres. At what is still the highest point of the European dramatic tradition, I look at a performance of Shakespeare's *Antony and Cleopatra*. I then take examples of the English drama in transition, from Wycherley's *The Plain Dealer*, in the Restoration, through Lillo's *The London Merchant*, in the eighteenth century, to Robertson's *Caste*, in the Victorian theatre. I follow this with a look at Stanislavsky's production, in the Moscow Art Theatre, of Chekhov's *The Seagull*: one of the high points of naturalism. I then look at three examples of modern experimental drama: T. S. Eliot's *The Family Reunion*, Bertolt Brecht's *The Life of Galileo*, and Samuel Beckett's *Waiting for Godot*. I conclude my particular examples with a look at a film: Ingmar Bergman's *Wild Strawberries*. I hope that the questions raised, in these particular examples, can then be brought together and restated, in a new way of looking at drama in performance.

# 2

## *Antigone,* by Sophocles: *c.* 442 B.C.

### THE CONDITIONS OF PERFORMANCE

THE occasion of the performance is the festival of the City Dionysia, in Athens, in the last days of March. On the first day of the festival, the image of Dionysus Eleuthereus was carried in a brilliant procession to a shrine outside the city, where a bull was sacrificed to it; after dark on that day, the image was carried back in a torchlight procession and placed in the theatre.

The whole dramatic festival is a ceremony of worship to Dionysus. Organized by the city, it will last for five days, during which three poets will each exhibit three tragedies and a satyric play, and there will also be performed five comedies and the singing, by boys' and men's choruses, of dithyrambic hymns. The work of the three poets, like the dithyrambic singing, is competitive; as is also the playing of the chief actor, or protagonist. The ceremonies of each day begin at dawn in the theatre, with a purifying sacrifice, and the offering of libations. In the centre of the front row of the auditorium is the priest of Dionysus Eleuthereus, and sitting beside him the priests of Zeus and Athena. Behind them are a huge audience, as many as seventeen thousand men, women and children. All business in the city is suspended while the festival lasts.

The theatre of Dionysus, in which this audience is now assembled, lies on the south-eastern slope below the rock of the Acropolis. To the west, the audience can see the city and the harbour; to the east, the open country. Below the auditorium, in which the audience sit on wooden seats up the terraced slope, the dominant feature is the circular *orchestra,* the dancing-place (*orchesis* = dancing). It is about sixty feet across, with a floor of beaten earth, and surrounded by a stone kerb. In the centre of the orchestra is an altar (*thymele*), with a step beside it. At the far side of the orchestra from the auditorium rises a wooden rectangular building, of one storey,

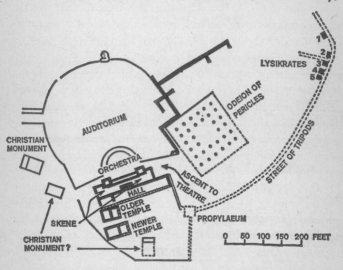

*Fig. 1.* Plan of the Theatre of Dionysus at Athens, and of its immediate environs.

about a hundred feet long. At each end of this building, wings (*paraskenia*) project towards the auditorium. Between these wings and the auditorium are two entrances to the orchestra (*parodoi*). The wooden building is known as the *skene,* and a wide central door opens from it on to the space between the projecting wings; doors also open on to this space from the wings themselves. The space is the *logeion,* the speaking-place for the actors, as opposed to the *orchestra,* the dancing-place for the chorus. The *logeion* is not a stage in the modern sense; it is raised about a foot above the level of the *orchestra*, in a broad step running back to the front of the *skene*. On this front is a painted scene, representing a palace. Behind the *skene* building is the temple and precinct of Dionysus, in which the image that is now in the theatre is normally kept.

The performance of each play is heralded by a trumpet, and in the *Antigone* the central door is opened, and the first actors enter the *logeion*. The play will be acted by three actors,

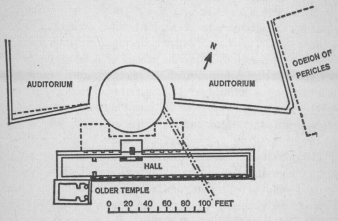

*Fig. 2.* Detail of playing-area, Theatre of Dionysus at Athens. The *skene* and *paraskenia* are indicated by the dotted line; and the space between the *paraskenia*, into which the circle of the *orchestra* projects, is the *logeion*.

who will share between them the individual speaking parts, and a chorus of fifteen, of whom the leader (*coryphaeus*) will also speak individually. Actors and chorus are all male. The actors wear a long robe, with a shorter over-mantle; these are richly coloured and decorated, but do not normally indicate character (except that a garment of open network may be worn to indicate a seer). On their feet the actors wear decorated shoes, with a thin sole (the shoes with soles of a thickness up to eight inches belong to a later period). The most significant feature of the actor's appearance is the mask he wears. This is made of cork and linen, and completely encloses his head. It is painted to represent character, the first distinction being white for female characters, and darker for males. The painting of the features is emphatic, and stylized, but not distorted. The eye-slits are left open, and the lips are parted.

The chorus is also masked, and its robes are decorated, although these remain much nearer normal dress than those of the actors. The chorus leader is distinguished by a greater degree of decoration. With the chorus is a flute player, in decorated costume, but unmasked. There are also, to supplement the actors, a number of additional performers, who are masked and dressed as the actors, but who will not speak.

For both actors and chorus, three kinds of delivery of words are available. These are, first, a mode of formal declamation, which is nearest to the mode of ordinary speech, but distinguished from it by the distinct emphasis of metre; second, a kind of recitative (*parakataloge*, as distinguished from *kataloge*, declamation), in which the chanting voice will be accompanied by the flute; and third, singing, again accompanied by the flute, either in the form of a solo (*monodia*), a duet or trio, singing between an actor and the chorus (*kommos*), or the ode of the whole chorus. The particular form of delivery employed at any point in the play is determined by the metre in which the lines to be delivered are written.

Gesture, accompanying the delivery of the words, is so far as possible indicated in the composition of the lines to be delivered. It is formal in character, and controlled from moment to moment by the words being delivered, 'as if the words and the parts of the body were connected by strings which the former pulled'. Dancing (*orchesis*), in its general sense, includes the use of the whole body, and especially the hands, as well as movements of the leg. The purpose of any movement is mimetic – that is to say, the physical realization of what is being verbally expressed, either by the person speaking or singing, or in response to what is being spoken or sung by another. There are three classes of movement: indications (the pointing of an object or person); motions (the expression of a feeling); and postures, *schemata* (the positions which may be held, and fixed, when a motion is complete). All these, as appropriate, will be employed by the actors, in the *logeion*. They will be employed also, in unison, by the chorus, in the *orchestra*. The chorus, which normally first enters the *orchestra* from the west, is formed into three files, each of five members of the chorus (*choreutæ*). The leader of the chorus is in the centre of the file which, when entering from the west, would be nearest to the audience; that is, in the centre of the front row. The flute player, who precedes the chorus in its entrance into the *orchestra*, then takes up his place on the step of the *thymele* in the centre. The chorus dance in that part of the *orchestra* nearest to the *logeion*.

These are the known conditions of performance. The trumpet has been sounded, and the performance of the *Antigone*, before this huge audience, gathered in the great open-air theatre for its most important religious festival, is about to begin. But before we look at parts of this performance, we need to look at Sophocles' text of the *Antigone*, which existed before the performance began, which controlled it during its realization, and which has survived both performance and theatre.

### THE TEXT

The text of the *Antigone* contains 1,353 lines of verse, in a variety of metres. It can be summarized, in terms of its action, so as to indicate its essential form. These, then, are the divisions:

*Lines 1–99*: PROLOGOS (the scene which precedes the entry of the chorus; originally a narrative soliloquy, the scene became a combination of narrative soliloquy and dialogue, but in Sophocles is always wholly dialogue).

*Antigone and Ismene, daughters of Oedipus, sisters of Eteokles and Polyneikes*

Antigone stresses the tragic destiny of their family, and the present situation is defined. Eteokles and Polyneikes are dead, at each other's hand; and although the invading Argive army has been driven away from Thebes, Polyneikes, who led it against his own city, is to suffer the indignity of being left unburied. This is the order of Kreon, the regent.

Antigone affirms that she will bury her brother, although the penalty for disobedience of the order is death; Ismene will not help her – the attempt is impossible.

*Lines 100–61*: PARODOS (the first song of the whole chorus; in this case, as commonly, the entrance song. Divided here into two strophes and two antistrophes; the antistrophes repeat the metrical patterns of the strophes. Lines 154–61 are in a different metre, and are an *indication* of the next character to enter).

*Chorus: the elders of Thebes*

The chorus greets the sun, the dawn of the morning of victory. The assault of the Argive army is rehearsed, and the victorious Theban defence, aided by Zeus; then the equal death of the contending brothers, Eteokles and Polyneikes. But now the fighting can be forgotten, and the city can rejoice.

Kreon approaches, and the elders are assembled to meet him.

## Antigone, *by Sophocles*

*Lines* 162–331: EPEISODION I (the first of the five central scenes of acted dialogue).

### *Kreon and Chorus* (ll. 162–222)

Kreon reminds the elders of their loyalty; with the death of Eteokles and Polyneikes, the sole kingship lies with him. He proclaims his edict that Polyneikes be left unburied and unmourned, because he led an invading army to destroy his own city. The elders confirm this as law, and swear to uphold it.

### *Kreon, Sentry and Chorus* (ll. 223–331)

The sentry, who has been placed with others to guard the body of Polyneikes, comes to announce that at dawn it was seen that the body had been strewn with dust, as a token of burial. The elders wonder if this has been done by the gods. Kreon repudiates this, and charges the sentry, on pain of death, to discover the 'author of this burial'.

*Lines* 332–84: STASIMON I (the first of the five choral odes sung by the chorus after it has taken up its position in the orchestra).

*Chorus* sings of the achievements of man; he travels the sea, and tills the earth; has established his mastery over all other creatures. He has learned, also, thought and language; and the way of living in cities, and by laws. To break these laws is to be cast out of human society and sympathy.

*Indication* (ll. 373–84): Antigone is being led in by the sentry.

*Lines* 385–581: EPEISODION II

### *Chorus, Sentry, Antigone,* (ll. 385–445)

The sentry has discovered Antigone in the act of burying

13

her brother's body. Antigone admits the act; Kreon sends away the sentry.

*Kreon, Antigone, Chorus* (ll. 446–526)

Kreon asks Antigone if she knew of the order against Polyneikes' burial. Antigone answers that she knew it, as everyone did, but that it was only a man-made law, and one which contradicted the 'unwritten laws, eternal in the heavens' that the dead should be honoured. Because this is so, she is even glad to die, honouring her dead brother. The chorus compares her stubbornness to that of her father, Oedipus. Kreon charges her with glorying in her crime, and orders that she must die.

*Ismene, Kreon, Antigone, Chorus* (ll. 527–81)

Ismene enters, and asks that she may share Antigone's guilt. Antigone refuses this. Ismene asks Kreon if he will kill the Antigone who was to marry his son Haemon; Kreon replies that her death will break the engagement. Antigone and Ismene are led, guarded, into the palace.

*Lines 582–630:* STASIMON II

*Chorus* sings of the doom that lies on this family of Oedipus; the curse never fails. The will of the gods is omnipotent; of man, against this, impotent.

*Indication* (ll. 628–30) of the approach of Haemon, son of Kreon, and betrothed to Antigone.

*Lines 631–780:* EPEISODION III
*Haemon, Kreon, Chorus* (ll. 631–763)

Haemon argues that the general opinion is against Kreon in this punishment of Antigone; Kreon angrily reaffirms that she must die. Haemon answers that he then will die with her.

14

*Kreon, Chorus* (ll. 764–80)

Kreon announces the manner of Antigone's death: she is
to be buried alive in a rock vault, with just enough food
to avert the guilt of murder.

*Lines 781–807:* STASIMON III

*Chorus* sings of the conquering power of love, and of
the conflict between Haemon's love of his father and of
Antigone.

*Indication* (ll. 801–7) of the approach of Antigone, being
led to her death. The chorus is overcome by pity.

*Lines 808–943:* EPEISODION IV

*Antigone, Chorus* (ll. 808–81) – KOMMOS

Antigone stresses her loneliness in the face of death, and
her awareness that she is working out the curse of her
unhappy family. The chorus reminds her that the crime
for which she is to die was her own self-willed act, even
although she is paying the price of her father's sin.

*Kreon, Antigone, Chorus* (ll. 882–943)

Kreon enters, and orders the mourning to end. Antigone
argues her fate, and is led away.

*Lines 944–87:* STASIMON IV

*Chorus* sings of others who have suffered the fate of being
buried alive, whose lot it was, the portion given them by
the grey spinners of fate, the Moirai.

*Lines 988–1114:* EPEISODION V

*Teiresias, Kreon, Chorus* (ll. 988–1090)

Teiresias, the blind prophet, comes to warn Kreon that
with Polyneikes unburied the city is polluted and the gods
angry. Kreon rejects the warning. Teiresias then prophesies
that for the death of Antigone, Kreon will pay with the life
of his own son.

*Kreon, Chorus* (ll. 1091–1114)

The chorus reminds Kreon that Teiresias has never falsely prophesied. Kreon at last retracts, and orders that Antigone be saved, and Polyneikes buried.

*Lines* 1115–53: STASIMON V

*Chorus* sings to the god of many names (Dionysus), that he may now heal the sickness of the city, and bring dancing and rejoicing.

*Lines* 1154–1353: EXODUS (literally the exit-song of the chorus; now the whole final scene, which in this case is complicated and critical).

*Messenger, Chorus* (ll. 1154–79): the messenger brings news that Haemon has killed himself in Antigone's burial vault.

*Eurydice, Messenger, Chorus* (ll. 1180–1243): Eurydice, mother of Haemon and wife of Kreon, hears the news and goes out silently.

*Chorus* (ll. 1244–56) fears the significance of the silence of Eurydice.

*Indication* (ll. 1257–60) of the approach of Kreon, bearing the body of Haemon in his arms.

*Kreon* (ll. 1261–9) sings a lament over Haemon; the chorus (l. 1270) replies. *Kreon* (ll. 1271–7) recognizes his folly.

*Messenger* (ll. 1278–83) enters to announce to Kreon that his wife Eurydice is also dead, in grief for Haemon.

*Kreon* (ll. 1284–93) again sings a lament for son and wife.

*Chorus, Kreon, Messenger* (ll. 1294–1344): the chorus indicates to Kreon the body of Eurydice, now shown in the palace. Kreon takes the whole guilt on himself, and asks to be led away.

*Chorus* (exit-song, ll. 1348–53) sings of wisdom and of reverence to the gods. An old man, taught by adversity, learns, too late, to be wise.

This is the end of the written play, and we may now turn again to its performance. It is worth considering how the parts may have been distributed among the three actors, although this cannot be certain. The distribution which I prefer is: first actor (protagonist) – Antigone and Eurydice; second actor (deuteragonist) – Ismene, Sentry, Haemon, Teiresias, Messenger; third actor (tritagonist) – Kreon. The doubling of roles was of course effected by a change of mask and, where appropriate, of voice.

## Lines 353–85

The first part of the play that I propose to examine in performance is that between lines 353 and 385. The situation at this point is that we already know Antigone's intention to bury her brother, in obedience to the unwritten law of reverence for the dead; and we know also Kreon's firmness in the order that he shall be left unburied, and the elders' assent to this. Further, we know that there has already been a token attempt at burial.

Now the essence of this conflict depends upon the active awakening of the feelings which have prompted both Antigone and Kreon in their wholly incompatible intentions. Kreon has argued the need to punish an enemy of the state, but the wider basis of this feeling is enacted by the hymn of the chorus in praise of the achievements of man, with the final stress on the sanctity of law.

The chorus is singing, and, through its dancing, acting the human achievement. This, in performance, is very much more than simple statement. The very fact that it comes from a chorus, a body of men moving together and singing in harmony, enacts part of the significance. Let us hear the second strophe and antistrophe of this chorus to Man:

Language, and thought like the wind
And the feelings that make the town
He has taught himself, and shelter against the cold,
Refuge from rain. He can always help himself.
He faces no future helpless. There's only death
That he cannot find an escape from. He has contrived
Refuge from illnesses once beyond all cure.

Clever beyond all dreams
The inventive craft that he has
Which may drive him one time or another to well or ill.
When he honours the laws of the land and the gods' sworn
    right
High indeed is his city; but stateless the man
Who dares to dwell with dishonour. Not by my fire,
Never to share my thoughts, who does these things.

The singing and dancing of this achievement of order is extraordinarily powerful, and it comes to a deliberate climax at which the intensity of the dramatic feelings is almost overpowering. For the gestures of the chorus, while they sing the last four lines, enact the contrast between the secure fidelity – 'high indeed is his city' – and the impassioned rejection of its opposite, the rejection of the human being who breaks the human law. As the chorus ends these lines, its collective gesture of rejection, of casting out the transgressor, fixes itself; it is drawn up in its ranks, holding the posture in which the motion of rejection ends, the held sign of casting out.

Now, at this point, the chorus is in the *orchestra*, facing the empty *logeion*. The ode has reached its climax, dramatically, in the posture of casting out. Then, into the logeion, comes the figure of Antigone, led by the sentry. The presence of the sentry at once establishes the fact of her attempt at the burial; she has deliberately disobeyed the law. But there is the white mask of Antigone, the mask of grief; and the hair is cut short, a reminder of her mourning. Thus both her motive, and the consequence of her act, are simultaneously, and actively, present. She stands guarded by the sentry; and the mask is fixed, in the expression of grief and mourning. But against this isolated mourning figure the arms of the chorus are still outstretched, in rejection of the breaker of laws.

Now the chorus leader steps forward, and the hands move from the gesture of rejection to an indication of Antigone, and an identification:

> My mind is split at this awful sight.
> I know her. I cannot deny
> Antigone is here.
> Alas, the unhappy girl,
> Her unhappy father's child.
> Oh what is the meaning of this?
> It cannot be you that they bring
> For breaking the royal law,
> Caught in open shame.

These lines are chanted, in *parakataloge*, with the flute in attendance. It is the transition, in itself dramatic, from the full song of the chorus back towards speech. While the chorus leader chants, the rest of the chorus, behind him, copy his agonized movements of doubt and grief. And 'her unhappy father's child': the element of fate in the crime is linked with the emotions of mourning and of rejection of the lawbreaker. The sentry leads Antigone forward; she moves slowly, her head bowed. The sentry speaks, the movement from song through recitative to speech now complete:

> This is the woman who has done the deed.
> We caught her at the burying.

The fact, thus bluntly delivered, settles, as it were, the whole pattern. All that has been feared and foreseen, all the conflict between the impulses of personal reverence and social law, is fixed now as the mourning Antigone faces the rejecting and horrified elders.

There are few passages in the whole extant Greek drama which exemplify so clearly the dramatic function of the means of performance. Kreon's statement of the sanctity of law (which will later, ironically, define his own fault) implants the idea; the hymn of the chorus enacts the feeling. Moreover, as the powerful social rejection of the lawbreaker is enacted, finding its unpremeditated and ultimately false object in the grieving mask of Antigone, there is an actual physical realization of the whole dramatic emotion. The chorus are many; the chorus is the group; and she is the solitary figure, guarded. And then in the realization of the situation, the intensity of the recitative is still available, assembling and enacting the relevant emotions. The masks of the old men; the mask of the guard; the grieving mask of Antigone: all reinforce the same pattern. And this, it is evident, is a known effect. Sophocles, working through the known conventions, has written the words so that they are necessarily enacted in this way, and with this issue. The words are the whole situation, for they contain and compel the intense physical realization.

## Lines 441–83

The lines examined are on the border of Stasimon I and Epeisodion II. To examine a different aspect of performance, we may now turn to lines 441–83, in which we can follow in detail a passage of acted dialogue. The situation is as formerly described, with the addition that the sentry has now described to Kreon how Antigone was caught in the attempt to bury Polyneikes.

Kreon is standing in the centre of the logeion; behind him are two mute attendants. The sentry, who has brought in Antigone, has advanced towards Kreon as he describes the capture. Antigone stands by the sentry, hanging her head.

KREON: You there, whose head is drooping to the ground,
    Do you admit this, or deny you did it?
ANTIGONE: I say I did it and I don't deny it.

In this question and answer, Kreon points to (*indicates*) Antigone as he speaks to her. She lifts her head, and answers clearly, but the words are simple. Kreon's pointing hand remains raised, in accusation. This position is held for a moment: Kreon, in his mask of the stern ruler, pointing the accusing hand; Antigone, who has been looking down, now having lifted her head and exposed the mask of mourning. Then:

KREON: Take yourself off wherever you wish to go.

The gesture of accusation of Antigone becomes a gesture of dismissal to the sentry. The sentry is freed from guilt, and goes, back through the door in the eastern *paraskenion* through which he brought Antigone. The accusation is now concentrated on Antigone alone:

KREON: You. Tell me not at length but in a word.
    You knew the order not to do this thing.

Kreon's words and actions, through all this questioning, are sharp and imperious. The pattern of gesture is simple, following the words: the accusation of Antigone; the dismissal of the sentry; the renewed accusation of Antigone. Antigone replies:

I knew, of course I knew. The word was plain.

As she speaks these words Antigone indicates, in gesture, the listening chorus, and beyond them the audience. But the point is brought sharply back to her alone, the accusing hand fixed:

KREON: And still you dared to overstep these laws?

The inclusive gesture of Antigone, acknowledging that she with the rest knew of the edict, remains in the memory to emphasize her present isolation. All is now concentrated on her, and she moves forward to speak at length, formally, in her own essential defence:

ANTIGONE: For me it was not Zeus who made that order.
  Nor did that Justice who lives with the gods below
  Mark out such laws to hold among mankind.
  Nor did I think your orders were so strong
  That you, a mortal man, could over-run
  The gods' unwritten and unfailing laws.
  Not now, nor yesterday's, they always live,
  And no one knows their origin in time.
  So not through fear of any man's proud spirit
  Would I be likely to neglect these laws,
  Draw on myself the gods' sure punishment.
  I knew that I must die; how could I not?
  Even without your warning. If I die
  Before my time, I say it is a gain.
  Who lives in sorrows many as are mine
  How shall he not be glad to gain his death?
  And so, for me to meet this fate, no grief.
  But if I left that corpse, my mother's son
  Dead and unburied I'd have cause to grieve
  As now I grieve not.

And if you think my acts are foolishness
The foolishness may be in a fool's eye.

Again, in this formally declaimed speech, the pattern of performance is clear. Antigone comes forward, under Kreon's pointed accusation. And at once, in words and gesture, she makes the distinction which is in fact the heart of the play's conflict. 'Not Zeus ... nor Justice ... your orders': the accusation is returned, as she points to Kreon alone. And again this is the precise pattern of the play, for as the action develops it is just this isolation of Kreon, who has acted against the laws of the gods, that becomes significant: 'the gods' unwritten and unfailing laws'. The appeal to an authority beyond Kreon is at once reinforced: 'they always live, and no one knows their origin in time'. It is a simple and very beautiful pattern, clear in words and action.

Antigone continues her defence. 'I knew that I must die. ... Who lives in sorrows many as are mine. ...' The concentration at this point is evident: the tormented, grieving mask; the movements of mourning and despair. But now comes the opposite movement, within the despair. 'If I left that corpse, my mother's son'. That is the intolerable alternative, now made present in the words and action. Against *that* 'now I grieve not'. And then she returns again to the counter-accusation: 'The foolishness may be in a fool's eye'.

Accusation and counter-accusation; Antigone no longer the quiet figure, with bowed head, but come forward, facing Kreon, and, by appealing to a higher authority, pointing accusingly at him. Again, the moment is held; and then the next element enters. The struggle is not between Kreon and Antigone alone; but between Antigone and the human law. Beyond Kreon is the chorus of elders, and now they speak:

The girl is bitter. She's her father's child.
She cannot yield to trouble; nor could he.

The isolation of Antigone is again emphasized, although now the isolation is defiant. Kreon, with the chorus behind him, makes the inevitable reply:

> These rigid spirits are the first to fall.
> The strongest iron, hardened in the fire,
> Most often ends in scraps and shatterings.
> Small curbs bring raging horses back to terms.

He has answered her with the naked assertion of power, and to emphasize this, he speaks now not to her alone, but generally; indicating thus her relative weakness.

> This girl was expert in her insolence
> When she broke bounds beyond established law.
> Once she had done it, insolence the second,
> To boast her doing, and to laugh in it.

The action will continue, but in this movement the decisive element of the pattern has been realized. Antigone now no longer bows her head; she is 'face to face'. She has returned the accusation on Kreon, even though the chorus has intervened. Against that corrupt power, the grieving girl can be intensely active, can seem even to rejoice. The action is intensely dramatic and immediate, but the method is so rich that every relevant emotion can not only be introduced, but made active. The spoken pattern and the physical pattern are one, and in their unity the pattern of the dramatic experience is realized.

*Lines 773–815*
To illustrate further how the written design of the play, and the physical pattern which this design controls, embodies with marvellous intensity the actual dramatic experience, we may next turn to lines 773–815. This passage will also show

a rather different kind of dramatic function in the relation of chorus and actors.

The passage comes at the end of Epeisodion III, in which the dominant action has been Haemon's appeal to his father to revoke the sentence of death on Antigone, and Kreon's rejection of this appeal. The explicit conflict here, as the argument between son and father grows fiercer, is between the reverence which as a son Hacmon must feel for his father, and the love which he has for Antigone, whom it was intended he would marry. Haemon leaves angrily, committing his father to 'other friends' who may approve his madness, and vowing that his father will never see him again. This committal and vow throw their shadows ahead, but Kreon, left with the chorus, turns to the announcement of the manner of Antigone's death:

> To take her where the foot of man comes not.
> There shall I hide her in a hollowed cave
> Living, and leave her just so much to eat
> As clears the city from the guilt of death.
> There if she prays to Death, the only god
> Of her respect, she may manage not to die.
> Or she may learn at last and even then
> How much too much her labour for the dead.

Kreon, having delivered his sentence, moves back, and the chorus moves forward in the orchestra, singing a single strophe and antistrophe:

Love unconquered in fight, love who falls on our havings.
You rest in the bloom of a girl's unwithered face.
You cross the sea, you are known in the wildest lairs.
Not the immortal gods can fly,
Nor men of a day. Who has you within him is mad.

You twist the minds of the just. Wrong they pursue and are
ruined.
You made this quarrel of kindred before us now.
Desire looks clear from the eyes of a lovely bride:
Power as strong as the founded world.
For there is the goddess at play with whom no man can fight.

This remarkable hymn to Love is of considerable dramatic
importance. Yet often, in commentaries on the play, it is said,
with an air that assumes the impossibility of disagreement,
that it is just a beautiful irrelevancy. The same comment has
been made, even more astonishingly, on the great hymn to
the achievements of Man in Stasimon I. The point about these
comments is that they show how, in an age dominated by
naturalistic attitudes to the drama, the dramatic functions of
a chorus of this type escape even expert notice. Either the
chorus makes a deliberate, explicit comment on the action,
or else, it is assumed, the choral ode is merely an interlude,
a piece of singing and dancing, perhaps beautiful in its own
terms. Certainly, in the decline of the Greek tragic drama,
the choral passages declined to the status of interludes. But in
a case like this, dramatic relevance is not to be construed in
terms of a comment on the 'story' or the 'problem'. A
choral ode like this is a dramatic realization of the pattern of
the whole play, a sudden intensification of its structure. One
could meet the point about irrelevance by drawing attention
to the function of the ode as a comment on the scene between
Haemon and Kreon: Haemon's love for Antigone conquering his necessary reverence for his father – 'this quarrel of
kindred'. But if this were the only point to be made, the
function could have been performed by a spoken intervention: commentary in the simplest sense. Yet this ode is sung
and danced: fifteen voices singing, fifteen dancers, by movement and gesture, creating and enacting its feelings. The

effect of this is not one which could have been obtained, in a different form, by a parenthetical comment, of the kind made by a novelist on a situation or a character.

The ode, when sung and danced, drawing on a maximum of rhythmic effect and intensity, creates as a *present* emotion, as real as any action, the whole moving tension between love and peace, love and order. The power of love against the power of law; the quickening of love, that contains within itself the potential of destruction and madness: these elements are an essential part of the structure of the whole of the *Antigone*. Nor are they merely stated, a comment thrown into the general progress of the argument. Because the dancing of the chorus is mimetic, because the sung words have a deliberate emotional intensity, the conflict is in fact enacted, made present, made to move. It is a conflict that has been played in action, in Antigone and Haemon; but now it is the play, as a whole, that is further enacting the struggle, at this point of intensity. The fear of love is enacted, but the fear only strikes when the power that is feared is physically apprehended. The dance of the chorus, following the sung words, is a physical pattern of the struggle between love and restraint.

The point is made clearer, and the possibility of regarding the ode as a mere interlude finally excluded, when we see what immediately follows. The chorus has sung, and is looking towards the empty *logeion*. Antigone enters, guarded, on her way to death. The leader of the chorus indicates her, and we hear his recitative:

> Now I am carried beyond all bounds.
> My tears will not be checked.
> I see Antigone depart.

It is a sudden, overcoming flood of feeling; a release, momentarily, from the calculation of law and guilt. Dramatically, it is a deliberate 'leading' of feeling towards Antigone, as a deepening of the tragic situation.

ANTIGONE: Men of my fathers' land, you see me go
　My last journey. My last sight of the sun . . .
　. . . Not for me was the marriage-hymn, nor will anyone start the song
　At a wedding of mine.

This death is the issue of love, of a love that overcame all governance. Now the whole pattern intensifies, as, in the succeeding *kommos* of seventy-six lines, Antigone sings of her death, and the chorus, singing its responses, recovers the arguments of order.

CHORUS: You showed respect for the dead.
　So we for you: but power
　Is not to be thwarted so.
　Your self-sufficiency has brought you down.
ANTIGONE: Unwept, no wedding-song, unfriended, now I go
　The road laid down for me.
　No longer shall I see this holy light of the sun.

The form of the *kommos*, the sung lamentation between protagonist and chorus, is the highest reach of the tragic experience which Greek drama embodies. It is not merely an abstract of the situation that the play offers, nor yet a description of it, nor merely a following through of action. The structure of the experience is isolated, and emphasized, in a sung intensity. The concentration of all the writing is upon the enacted pattern, and the singing voices and the moving hands, the moving pattern in the open space, under the high auditorium, are one.

## CONCLUSION

The point made about the chorus song in Stasimon III is equally true of all the choral songs in the play: Stasimon II, with its images of storm and fire, rehearsing the destruction of a house that is cursed; Stasimon IV, when Antigone has gone out to her death, enacting the horror of being buried alive by recalling others who have suffered it, and rehearsing their fate; Stasimon V, when after the intervention of Teiresias, Kreon has at last retracted, and the chorus breaks into the hymn to Dionysus, the cleansing, the rejoicing of the dance. In the case of this last, the song to the god in whose honour the play is performed, the chorus enact a rejoicing which immediately precedes the tragic climax, and deeply affects it by contrast: an effect similar to that of Stasimon I, where the call to rejoicing at the relief of the city follows the scene in which Antigone has made clear the essential tragic situation. The more one looks at the text of the play, the more one realizes that a simple, yet radical, pattern, a controlling structure of feeling, has been clearly isolated and designed in the writing. And then, if one looks at the performance, one sees that this design is being continually enacted, in the parts as in the whole. For it is a design made for performance; the purpose of the play is not report, not description, not analysis, but enactment of a design. The structure of feeling is the formal written structure, and also the structure of performance. The conflict and resolution are not a story, a telling of things past, but are always present, in words and movement.

It is necessary to emphasize this, because a reader might easily conclude that the play is essentially over, or at least has reached its climax, when Antigone is led out to her death.

But the design has a continuing intensity, and it is in the final tragic realization of Kreon that the authentic climax is reached. Kreon has rejected Teiresias' advice, but he bows, reluctantly, to his threatening prophecy, that Haemon also will die. He hurries out to save Antigone, and orders that Polyneikes be buried. The chorus sings the hymn to Dionysus, the wished-for cleansing, so that at last the city may dance. But then the first Messenger enters, with the news that Haemon has died with Antigone; Haemon's mother, Eurydice, hears of her son's death, and goes out in silence to take her own life. Kreon re-enters, carrying the body of Haemon. This final scene – the second *kommos* of the play – has a deliberate stillness, almost a sculptured quality. Kreon stands, with Haemon's body in his arms, and now no longer speaks, but sings his lament:

> You see the killer, you see the kin he killed . . .

The chorus answer him, and he replies (both perhaps in recitative), and then the news of Eurydice's death is brought from the palace. The central door in the *skene* opens, and the body of Eurydice is seen, lying there in death. The chorus indicates it:

> Now you can see. Concealment is all over.

Kreon, still standing, again sings his lament:

> My second sorrow is here. Surely no fate remains
> Which can strike me again.

As Kreon stands thus, the Messenger, incisively, adds the details of Eurydice's death; and Kreon, utterly broken, asks to be led away:

> Servants, take me away, out of the sight of men.
> I who am nothing more than nothing now . . .

... Let me go, let me go. May death come quick
Bringing my final day ...
... I cannot rest.
My life is warped past cure. My fate has struck me down.

This writing makes inevitable the hopeless, turning appeal:

> Let me go, let me go ...
> ... I cannot rest.

Still bearing the body of Haemon, moving slowly under the burden, the head bowed, this 'fate too heavy for me', he is led in beside the body of his wife, and slowly the central door of the palace closes.

The *logeion* is again empty, and the chorus stand in the *orchestra*. The flute player comes down from the *thymele*, and as the chorus turn, takes his place at the head of them. They move out slowly towards the western *parodos*, the lines of figures, masked as old men. As they go, they chant, with the flute accompanying them, in recitative:

> Our happiness depends
> On wisdom all the way.
> The gods must have their due.
> Great words by men of pride
> Bring greater blows upon them.
> So wisdom comes to the old.

They pass out of sight, the orchestra is empty, and the play has ended.

# 3

# English Medieval Drama

(*The Three Maries*: c. 1300; *Abraham, Melchisedec, and Isaac*: c. 1327; *Secunda Pastorum*: c. 1475; *Everyman*: c. 1495)

THE English medieval drama offers a number of important and unique features in the study of performance; but its extent in time, over nearly four centuries, and the wide degree of local variation, make it necessary to illustrate these by consideration of the elements of a number of plays, rather than by concentration on one single work.

## 'THE THREE MARIES'

The scene here called *The Three Maries* is part of a great Cornish trilogy. The three major parts are *Origo Mundi*; *Passio Domini*; *Resurrexio Domini*; and the range of the whole action extends from the Creation to Christ's Ascension into Heaven. Many very similar works existed in French and Anglo-Norman literature, and there are important earlier examples in medieval Latin. Each part of the trilogy occupied a day in performance; the three parts were played on consecutive days, before an audience drawn from the surrounding countryside. The *Origo Mundi* contains 2,824 lines; the *Passio Domini* 3,216; and the *Resurrexio Domini* 2,630. The episode here called *The Three Maries* comprises the *Quem Quaeritis* (ll. 679–834) and the *Hortulanus* (ll. 835–92) of the *Resurrexio Domini*, which was performed on the third day.

The place of performance was known as a *plen an gwary* (the plays are often later referred to as Guary miracles, or

Guirremears). This was a large circular arena, or *round*, varying in diameter from fifty to one hundred and twenty-six feet. A terraced bank of earth, and in some places rows of stone seats, enclosed the round; and here the spectators sat. Within the round there was a central circular playing-space, known as the *platea*, and later as the *playne*. (*Platea* is sometimes translated as 'stage', but, for this period, it is the open space that must be emphasized.) Around the *platea* was a ring of eight *pulpita*, or *tenti*. These represented certain fixed points in the action of each day.

On the day of the *Resurrexio Domini*, the eight *pulpita* represent *Celum, Tortores, Infernum, Pilatus, Imperator, Joseph, Nichodemus, Milites*. Each place was clearly defined, either, in the case of heaven or hell, by a degree of symbolical representation (a raised scaffold for heaven, a dragon's mouth for hell), or, in other cases, by association with particular characters. They might be called, in a limited, pre-theatrical sense of the word, *stages* – that is to say, places to which the action moved; they were later called *scaffolds* and *rooms*. In performance, the characters played either at one of these *pulpita*, where the action was relevant, or moving about in the open *platea*, where certain other representations (the cross, the sepulchre) would, in the course of the action, be set up. The *Resurrexio Domini* includes scenes of the release of Joseph and Nichodemus, played at their defined places; of Christ's Harrowing of Hell, played at the *Infernum*; of the setting of the watch at the sepulchre, set in the *platea*, perhaps between the *Celum* and the *Infernum*; of the rising from the sepulchre; of the coming of the Three Maries to find the stone rolled away and Christ risen; of Mary Magdalene meeting Christ in the near-by garden, played in the *platea*; of her report to the apostles, the unbelief of Thomas, and the appearance of Christ to the travellers to Emmaus, again played in the *platea*; of the death of Pilate, played at his defined place; and finally of the

Ascension, when Christ would go up from the *platea* into the *Celum*. The method of the action is, then, a combination of the use of defined places, in which either symbolic representation or association with a character establishes locality, and the creation of locality by the words and action, in the open neutral playing-space. The essential design of the whole cycle is the *movement* from the Creation, through the Passion and Resurrection, to the Ascension; and the method of performance is, in its main outlines, a similar design of movement; the action, at its crises, physically embodying the dramatic development.

In the episode which we are calling *The Three Maries*, the characters are Mary Magdalene, Mary the mother of James, and Mary Salome, with two angels, and the gardener who is the risen Christ. The women gather at the tomb, and mourn, and the angels appear to them to announce the resurrection. Mary Magdalene is left by the tomb, alone, and then goes into the garden, where she meets the gardener who reveals himself to her as Jesus. The formal pattern of this mourning at the tomb is very beautiful. The three women speak alternately, and together sing a lament. They are moving now across the *platea* towards the sepulchre:

> MARY SALOME: So with me is sorrow;
>    May the Lord see my state
>    After him.
>    As he is head of sovereignty
>    I believe that out of the tomb
>    Today he will rise.
>
> MARY MAGD.: Oh let us hasten at once,
>    For the stone is raised
>    From the tomb.
>    Lord, how will it be this night,
>    If I know not where goes
>    The head of royalty?

MARY, M. JAMES: And too long we have stayed,
My Lord is gone his way
Out of the tomb, surely.
Alas, my heart is sick;
I know not indeed if I shall see him
Who is very God.

One can see the essential movement of the design of these lines, in the stages of approach to the tomb: *I believe that . . . he will rise; let us hasten . . . the stone is raised; too long we have stayed . . . my Lord is gone his way.* But the design is also that of the three voices, which we find so often in medieval drama, and which is now repeated at the tomb itself. The three women sing together:

Alas, mourning I sing, mourning I call
Our Lord is dead that bought us all.

MARY MAGD.: Alas it is through sorrows
My sweet Lord is dead
Who was crucified.
He bore without complaining
Much pain on his dear body
For the people of the world.

MARY, M. JAMES: I cannot see the form
Of him on any side;
Alas, woe is me.
I would like to speak with him
If it were his will,
Very seriously.

MARY SALOME: There is to me sharp longing
In my heart always,
And sorrow.
Alas, my Lord Jesus,

For thou art full of virtue,
All mighty.
    Alas, mourning I sing, mourning I call,
    Our Lord is dead that bought us all.

The design here is a kind of dramatic action which some modern definitions of action would altogether exclude: the action of a structure of feeling, expressed in a rhythmic pattern of dramatic speech, at a gained point of stillness and intensity.

These are two of the important elements of performance in this kind of resurrection play: the design of movement towards a known physical place, which is the essential dramatic structure of these plays, developed, though with critical changes, from the processional liturgy; and the design of *celebration*, when the place is attained. There is yet a third element, in a kind of action which is perhaps more familiar to us: the meeting of characters. Mary Magdalene is left alone, and, after speaking, goes back into the *platea*, where she meets Jesus disguised as the gardener (the dramatic locality of the garden is of course created solely by the gardener's character):

GARDENER: O woeful woman . where goest thou?
  For grief thou prayest . cry out thou dost.
  Weep not nor shriek . he whom thou seekest
  Thou didst dry his feet . with thy two plaits.
MARY MAGD.: Good Lord . if thou hast chanced to see
  Christ my saviour . where is he truly?
  To see him . I give thee my hand;
  Jesus, son of grace . hear my desire.
GARDENER: O Mary . as I know thee to be
  Within this world . one of his blood
  If thou shouldst see him . before thee
  Couldst thou . know him?
MARY MAGD.: Well I do know . the form
  Of the son of Mary . named Jesus;

Since I see him not . in any place
I feel sorrow . else would I not sing alas!

GARDENER: Mary see . my five wounds
Believe me truly . to be risen
To thee I give thanks . for thy desire.
Joy in the land . there shall be truly.

MARY MAGD.: O dear Lord . who wast on the cross tree
To me it becomes not . to kiss thy hand
I would pray thee . let me dare
Now to kiss . once thy feet

GARDENER: O woeful woman . touch me not near
No it will not serve . nor be for gain
The time is not come.
Until I go . to heaven to my Father
And I will return . again to my country
To speak with thee

MARY MAGD.: Christ, hear my voice . say the hour. ...

The pattern of the speech is very clear and simple, with its
deliberate balance, as in the earlier scenes. But there is also a
new element, for this is acted speech between persons, and one
has only to listen to the lines to see how they contain the
action, crystallizing a pattern of gesture and movement on
each side. *Where goest thou? ... Where is he truly?; hear my
desire ... O Mary; before thee ... I see him not, in any place ...
Mary see: my five wounds ... I would pray thee; to kiss once thy
feet ... touch me not near; until I go to heaven, to my Father.*
These are the key phrases of the physical encounter, not only
containing movement within themselves, but forming a
physical design which corresponds to the whole spoken design.
Christ's revelation – *Mary see* – has a simple, clear intensity
which is an authentic crisis, and which the whole movement
supports. Certainly the patterns of such drama are simple, the
realization of a known faith; but within the simplicity, what

37

we find is not a primitive dramatic mode, but a distinct kind of maturity. As had happened before, in the movement from Greek ritual to the new and distinct form of drama, so elements and conventions of what was once a liturgical procession in the Church have, over centuries, been developed into a new, separate and self-sufficient dramatic form.

## ENGLISH MIRACLE PLAYS: 'ABRAHAM, MELCHISEDEC, AND ISAAC'; AND 'SECUNDA PAGINA PASTORUM'.

The performance of the Cornish miracle plays depended upon a number of fixed *stations* within a single place, the *plen an gwary*. The form of the plays corresponds, for they are essentially continuous cycles, moving from place to place within the round as the action requires. In many other parts of England, in the fourteenth and fifteenth centuries, the plays were also arranged as cycles. Many of these miracle plays, and nearly all the later moralities and interludes, were performed as 'standing plays'; that is to say, on a fixed playing space, in which certain *stations* or *sedes* were marked by scaffolds, or other fixed structures, on the same principle as in the Cornish performances, and indeed in the great majority of similar performances in the rest of Europe. But also, a new method of performance emerged, as a result of combining the performance of the plays with one of the great processions of the religious festivals. At Whitsun, and especially on Corpus Christi day, plays from a religious cycle would be allotted individually to particular trade guilds: e.g. *The Fall of Lucifer*, to the Tanners; *The Last Supper*, to the Bakers; *The Day of Judgement*, to the Websters. Each guild would then mount its own play on a *pagina*, or *pageant*, which is described by an eye-witness as 'a highe place made like a howse with ij rowmes, beinge open on ye tope: the lower rowme they apparelled and dressed them selves; and in the higher rowme they played; and they stood upon 6 wheeles'. This is a difficult physical structure to realize, and it is probably best to think of it as a movable stage. These may have been moved in procession (there is some evidence for this), from place to place in the town, with repeated performances. Or, in other cases, there would be a series of pageants, and the actors would move from one to the other. On the day of the festival, performances would begin in the early morning, with the first play of the cycle being performed on a pageant at the first of a number of known stations in the streets. In either kind of performance, the place in front of the pageant – usually the open street or square – would also be used for important parts of the action. In York there appear to have been as many as sixteen stations; in Coventry as few as four.

We can look briefly at the scene of the sacrifice of Isaac from the play *Abraham, Melchisedec, and Isaac,* which is the fourth of the twenty-five pageants played at Chester, and is performed by the Barbers and Wax-Chandlers. The performance is on Whit-Monday, when nine pageants are played; nine will follow on the next day; and seven on the third. It is now at the first station, before the gates of the Abbey; scaffolds are set up to accommodate the spectators, who surround the pageant on three sides.

The Messenger appears on the pageant:

> All peace, Lordings, that be present,
> And hearken now with good intent,
> How Noah away from us he went
> With all his company . . .

(the pageant of Noah and the Deluge had immediately preceded this, and has now gone to play at the second station – at the high cross before the Mayor)

... And Abraham, through God's grace
He is come forth into this place
And you will give him room and space
To tell you his storye.
This play forsooth begin shall he
In worship of the Trinity
That you may all hear and see
What shall be done today.

The Messenger goes, and Abraham enters, in front of the pageant. The first scenes are between Abraham and Lot, and then Abraham and Melchisedec; the Expositor comments on Melchisedec's gift to Abraham, which he sees as the New Testament and the sacrament of communion. Then God, on the pageant, appears to Abraham, and commands him to sacrifice Isaac. Isaac enters:

ABRAHAM: Make thee ready, my darling,
  For we must do a little thing.
  This wood upon thy back thou bring,
  We must not long abide.
  A sword and fire I will take,
  For sacrifice I must make;
  God's bidding will I not forsake
  But aye obedient be.
ISAAC: Father, I am all ready
  To do your bidding meekly,
  To bear this wood full bound am I
  As you command me.
ABRAHAM: ... Now Isaac, son, go we our way
  To yonder mountain, if that we may.

The ascent to the mountain is performed by moving from the open space on to the pageant itself; and it is there that the subsequent scene of some 165 lines is played. Abraham binds Isaac for the sacrifice, and then:

ABRAHAM: Lord, I would fain work thy will.
This young innocent that lies so still
Full loth were I him to kill
By any manner of way.

ISAAC: My dear father, I you pray,
Let me take my clothes away
For shedding blood on them today
At my last ending.

ABRAHAM: Heart, if thou wouldst break in three,
Thou shalt never master me
I will no longer let for thee,
My God I may not grieve.

ISAAC: Ah mercy, father! why tarry you so?
Smite off my head, and let me go!
I pray you, rid me of my woe!
For now I take my leave.

ABRAHAM: Ah son, my heart will break in three
To hear thee speak such words to me.
Jesus, on me thou have pity
That I have most in mind.

ISAAC: Now, father, I see that I shall die.
Almighty God in majesty
My soul I offer unto thee.
Lord, to it be kind.

Abraham raises the sword above the still body of Isaac, but two angels appear above him, and one seizes the point of the sword and holds it. The sacrifice is spared, and the ram is substituted. Then God appears again to Abraham, and commends him. The Expositor follows, and sees the significance of the event as an example of God's sacrifice of His own son Jesus on the cross.

This kind of miracle play is very simple dramatically, but the speech between Abraham and Isaac shows the capacity of this drama to concentrate, at an attained point in the action, on a simple pattern of feeling, expressed through a rhythmic pattern of dramatic speech. Of all the elements in medieval drama, this capacity for concentration on a pattern is, I think, the most important. But the visual representation would have a very important effect: the appearance of God the Father, in his traditional coat of white leather, and perhaps (as was sometimes the case) masked; the sudden appearance of the angels, dressed again in white, their wings spread, and the outspread arm to hold the sword. The physical representation of the known figures and images of a faith has a clear intensity, in direct relation to the known beliefs of the audience. The whole motive of such drama is, essentially, *celebration*.

As this kind of drama developed, elements of what would now be called realism made their appearance: scenes drawn directly from contemporary everyday life, combined with the celebration of known religious scenes. The most remarkable example of this development is the well-known *Secunda Pastorum* (the Second Pageant of the Shepherds) from the Towneley cycle, which has associations with the neighbourhood of Wakefield. I want to make only one comment on this play: a point about performance, which allows us to see its structure more clearly. The *Secunda Pastorum* may have been performed on the movable *pagina*, but I think it is more likely that it is a 'standing play'. In either case, however, there is an element of its structure which can be fully realized only when performance is considered. The religious act of the play is the calling of the Shepherds to Bethlehem, and their worship of the Christ child. Combined with this is an act of sheep stealing, in which Mac, a notorious thief, takes a 'fat wether' from the shepherds' flock. To hide the theft, his wife takes the animal into her bed, and pretends it is her new-born child. The treatment of this part is remarkable for its vitality, and has often been praised on these grounds. Some writers, indeed, see the episode as 'the beginning of a real dramatic sense' – a comment based on modern assumptions that drama is essentially the realistic representation of everyday individual characters. The realism is obvious, but if we think of the performance of the play, we see the same essential element of pattern which has already been described. The shepherds come in search of their wether, and Mac's wife groans, with the animal hidden beside her. And it is in the offering of a gift to the child that the fraud is detected:

> The child will it not grieve, that little day starn.
> Mac, with your leave, let me give your bairn
>   But Sixpence.

The offering of a gift, to the mother in her childbed, by the three shepherds, is, of course, not only an element in this episode, but relates directly to the later offering in the stable:

> Hail, little tiny mop,
> Of our creed thou art crop!
> I would drink in thy cup,
> Little day starn.

In performance, the repetition of the movement and the offering would be evident; it seems certain that the place where Mac's wife lies with the sheep would be identical with that where the Virgin nurses the Christ child. As in all this drama, the action creates the place and the feeling. And what is then significant is that the new dramatic interest is achieved by a repetition and variation of a familiar pattern. The realism of the shepherds is defined by the general pattern to which they finally refer.

### 'EVERYMAN'

We can now consider briefly the performance of a different and later kind of medieval play, the *Summoning of Everyman*,

which is what we now call a *morality*. The change in dramatic
method is that the characters represent abstract qualities –
*Strength*, *Beauty*, *Knowledge* – rather than names from the
Christian story. *Everyman* is a play of about 900 lines of verse;
it is introduced by a Messenger, and its significance explained
by a Doctor. The action is the summoning of Everyman by
Death, God's messenger, and the testing by Everyman of the
value of a number of human qualities, as in this final moment
they appear.

The essential elements for the performance of the play are a
*platea*, or open playing-space, of the Cornish kind although
not necessarily circular; and in the centre of it, a scaffold, two
storeys high, with the lower 'room' covered, and the higher
open at the top – this scaffold is the 'House of Salvation'.
The lower, covered room represents the grave; the higher is
heaven. A ladder runs between the two storeys. The action
begins from the scaffold, and ends on it; the intermediate
action is mainly in the open playing-space, where at least two
other dramatic *sedes* – for *Goods* and *Good Deeds* – are sited,
probably directly opposite each other, and some yards in front
of the scaffold. The audience surrounds the playing-space on
three sides.

The Messenger begins, speaking from the front of the *platea*:

> I pray you all give your audience
> And hear this matter with reverence,
> By figure a moral play . . .
> For ye shall hear, how our Heaven King
> Calleth Everyman to a general reckoning:
> Give audience, and hear what he doth say.

He is indicating the upper room of the scaffold, where God
now appears:

> I perceive here in my majesty
> How that all creatures be to me unkind

44

Living without dread in worldly prosperity:
Of ghostly sight the people be so blind.

The whole of this speech turns on the repetition of *I perceive* . . .
*I see*; it is God looking out from his high place and judging the
sins of the world below. At last he summons Death, who comes
up to him from the lower room. The figure of God is the
traditional image – the white leather coat, and the masked
head; the figure of Death is black, masked with a skull. God
commands Death to fetch Everyman, and Death replies:

Lord, I will in the world go run over all . . .

(he is indicating the *platea* and the audience below), and then:

Lo, yonder I see Everyman walking . . .

(Everyman has entered the *platea*, from the direction of the
audience, and now Death goes down to the lower room again,
and then emerges to confront Everyman):

Everyman, stand still; whither art thou going
Thus gaily?

The pattern, and the immediate dramatic effect, of this action
(reinforced by the physical creation of Heaven, the Grave and
the World – the upper and lower rooms and the *platea*) is
intense and clear. Everyman is confronted by death:

O Death, thou comest when I had thee least in mind.

As Death convinces him that the summons is inescapable, he
looks up to the higher room of the scaffold, where his eyes
have not previously been directed; he addresses God, who is
seated there, looking down:

O gracious God, in the high seat celestial,
Have mercy on me in this most need.

45

Shall I have no company from this vale terrestrial
Of mine acquaintance that way me to lead?

If the play is read, without consideration of the conditions of performance, a speech of this kind (like the previous speeches of God and Death) may appear to be an abstract appeal, with no realizable dramatic relation. It is written, however, for the actual dramatic realization we have described; the physical design corresponds exactly to the design of the verbal pattern. This may be seen throughout the play.

Death now leaves Everyman

– And now out of thy sight I will me hie

– and returns to the covered lower room. Everyman is alone in the *platea*:

Now have I no manner of company
To help me in my journey.

He turns, and looks for support. In turn now he summons aid, and is rejected:

... Fellowship ...
I see him yonder, certainly;

Where be ye now, my friends and kinsmen?

My Cousin, will you not with me go?

In turn, these enter and speak with him, in the *platea*, but all go back towards the world, and away from the house of death and salvation. Everyman, again alone, turns to his Goods (the character of *Goods*, encumbered as he describes, is already lying at his place):

Where art thou, my Goods and riches?

Who calleth me? Everyman? what haste thou hast!
I lie here in corners, trussed and piled so high,

46

> And in chests I am locked so fast
> Also sacked in bags, thou mayest see with thine eye,
> I cannot stir.

There is no one to walk with Everyman here. And the same is true when he turns in the opposite way, and calls on his Good-Deeds:

> My Good-Deeds, where be you?

> Here I lie cold in the ground;
> Thy sins hath me sore bound,
> That I cannot stir.

It is, I think, very remarkable, this physical, and wholly dramatic, expression of a crisis of the soul. Fellowship and Kindred can walk, but walk away, back towards the world and the audience. Goods and Good-Deeds, if for different reasons, cannot move at all, in this necessary journey. But now Knowledge, the sister of Good-Deeds, rises to accompany Everyman; it is knowledge, in these first encounters, that Everyman has gained:

> Everyman, I will go with thee, and be thy guide,
> In thy most need to go by thy side.

And they go together in search of Confession, who dwells

> In the house of salvation:
> We shall find him in that place.

They approach the lower room, and the character of Confession emerges from it, standing as it were at the edge of death and of salvation:

> Lo, this is Confession; kneel down and ask mercy.

Everyman kneels, and is given penance. He then prays to his God above –

> O eternal God, O heavenly figure.

Knowledge stands beside him, the means of his redemption. And now Everyman rises, and receives from Knowledge

the scourge of penance

(this is not a figure, but an actual scourge:

Everyman . . .
*Thus* I bequeath you in the hands of our Saviour,
*Thus* may you make your reckoning sure).

The same dramatic process is then repeated, for as Everyman accepts penance, Good-Deeds, who had formerly lain 'cold in the ground'

. . . can walk and go
. . . delivered of my sickness and woe.

Good-Deeds rises and comes to stand also beside Everyman:

KNOWLEDGE: Now is your Good-Deeds whole and sound
  Going upright upon the ground.

Everyman, below the House of Salvation, has now both Knowledge and Good-Deeds at his side. And as Knowledge had given him the scourge of penance, so now Good-Deeds gives him

a garment of sorrow
From pain it will you borrow;
Contrition it is,
That getteth forgiveness.

He is told to 'put on this garment . . . which is wet with your tears', and does so:

For now have I on true contrition.

In his new condition, he is advised to summon his particular friends – Discretion, Strength, Beauty and Five-wits. He calls

them, and they come out across the *platea* and gather around
him, to support him in his pilgrimage. He is advised by
Knowledge to seek a priest to receive the sacrament, and he
goes to do this, while the others wait for his return. (It is
probable that Everyman goes at this time to another 'fixed
point', rather than again to the House of Salvation. He may
even go right out of sight of the audience, and then return, for
the giving of the sacrament is not represented. And when he
returns:

> FIVE-WITS: Peace, for yonder I see Everyman come,
>    Which hath made true satisfaction.
> GOOD-DEEDS: Methinketh it is he indeed.

This is clearly an approach from some distance, and Everyman
has certainly been out of sight. The reason against his entering
the covered lower room of the House of Salvation becomes
apparent in the next scene.)

When Everyman is back, with all his qualities grouped
around, and still wearing the garment of contrition, he enters
at last upon his final journey. With the group supporting him,
and each setting his hand upon the cross which Everyman
now carries, he moves towards the House of Salvation, and
approaches the covered lower room in which is Death:

> Alas! I am so faint I may not stand,
> My limbs under me do fold;
> Friends, let us not turn again to this land

(he indicates the whole playing-space and the audience behind
him)

> Not for all the world's gold.
> For into this cave must I creep

(he indicates the covered lower room)

> And turn to the earth and there to sleep.

But now, at this last stage of the journey, Beauty leaves him –

> I take my cap in my lap and am gone;

Strength leaves him –

> I will hie me from thee fast;

Discretion leaves him –

> When Strength goeth before
> I follow after evermore;

Five-wits leaves him –

> I will follow the other, for here I thee forsake.

Even Knowledge will finally forsake him –

> But not yet for no manner of danger . . .
> Till I see where ye shall be come.

Only Good-Deeds will go with him all the way:

> All fleeth save Good-Deeds, and that am I . . .
> Fear not, I will speak for thee . . .
> Let us go and never come again.

And Everyman, below the House of Salvation, lifts up his hands to God:

> Into thy hands, Lord, my soul I commend.

With Good-Deeds beside him, he enters the 'cave' of Death – the covered lower room – and disappears. Knowledge is left in view, and turns to the audience:

> Now hath he suffered that we all shall endure.
> The Good-Deeds shall make all sure.
> Now hath he made ending.
> Methinketh that I hear angels sing

And make great joy and melody
Where Everyman's soul received shall be.

The action returns now to the upper room where it began.
There is a song of angels, and an angel appears, high on the
upper room, looking down into the 'cave of Death';

Come, excellent elect spouse to Jesu:
Hereabove thou shalt go.

And so Everyman, having passed through Death, comes out
at last into the presence of his God, in the upper room of the
House of Salvation:

Unto the which

(adds the angel, as he appears, and speaking out now to the
whole audience)

all ye shall come
That liveth well before the day of doom.

The climax is reached, and the Doctor ends the play with a
committal:

Unto which place God bring us all thither
That we may live body and soul together.
Thereto help the Trinity,
Amen, say ye, for sainte Charity.

As we follow the detailed performance of *Everyman*, we find
not only a masterpiece of literature (as which it has been often
praised), but a masterpiece of *dramatic* literature. All the elements of drama – speech, movement and design – concentrate
into a single pattern. The dramatic imagination of the 'ab-
stractions' is so clear that we no longer want to say that the
morality play is pre-dramatic, just because it uses types rather
than individuals. For a compelling feeling, at once individual
and general, has been realized in a fully dramatic pattern,

where speech, action and design are one. I would emphasize again the conception of Good-Deeds, at first 'lying cold in the ground', and then, after Everyman's confession, able to walk and support him; or, in design, the compelling beauty of the final movement through the dark 'cave' of Death into the open light of salvation. This is physically enacted, and not merely reported; and the same is true of the whole moral pattern, which is not in any way abstract, but is wholly and vitally present and actual. Our approach to a play like *Everyman* is then not to a specimen of a primitive dramatic mode; but, rather, to recognition of a highly developed kind of drama, in which there is an organic connection between dramatic feeling and dramatic method. While that structure of feeling held, this kind of drama was not a forerunner, but was already mature.

# 4

## *Antony and Cleopatra,* by Shakespeare: *c.* 1607

### THE CONDITIONS OF PERFORMANCE

THE performance is in the Globe Theatre, on Bankside, south of the Thames. The Globe is one of a number of theatres in which performances are given, since the first English public theatre was built in 1576. The company at the Globe is the King's Men, formerly the Lord Chamberlain's Men. Each company has a wide repertory of its own plays, and as many as twenty can be presented in a single season. The King's Men perform not only in the Globe – a London public theatre – but often during the winter at Court, and in a variety of places during their frequent tours. In the Globe, performances begin at two o'clock in the afternoon; and, when successful, attract an audience of between one and two thousand people.

The Globe Theatre is a wooden building, probably polygonal in its outer walls, and round within. The Fortune Theatre, which was closely modelled on the Globe, but which was shaped square, measured eighty feet each way overall, and fifty-five feet each way in its interior. The whole interior of the theatre – that is to say, including both auditorium and stage – is about the size of the *orchestra* in the Theatre of Dionysus at Athens.

The theatre is between thirty and forty feet high, and has galleries, in three storeys, running all around its walls. Within these galleries is the yard, into which the stage projects.

The stage is some forty feet wide, and extends into the middle of the yard, giving a depth of some twenty-seven feet. The spectators, in the galleries and the yard, surround the stage on three sides. The height of the stage above the level of the yard is about six feet. The galleries are roofed over with thatch, but the yard is open to the sky. Over the stage, however, extends a cover, known as the 'heavens' or 'shadow', beginning a little below the eaves of the top gallery, and probably sloping forward, and supported by two tall pillars towards the front of the stage.

At the back of the stage is the Tire-House, where the actors prepare themselves. From this there are two doors, one on either side, affording entrance to the stage. Between the doors, there is an arras, or hanging curtain. Above this, and projecting slightly over the open stage, is a gallery, which is available on occasion for the action of the play. It is some ten or twelve feet above the main stage, and is accessible from behind by means of stairs from the tiring-room. On the main stage there are three or four trap-doors, large enough for properties to be drawn up through them, when necessary, from the space below the stage.

Scenic representation, on this stage, is functional but often striking. A painted backcloth can be used, for the panorama of a city; battlements can be set up (the gallery is already available as the wall of a city or a castle); a window can be set in the gallery (which is thus available for the upper room of a house); a hell's mouth can be set in an open trap; alcoves, bowers, cells, tombs can be disposed on the platform, for any particular action; trees, where necessary, can be set on the stage, and mossy banks; and such ordinary furnishings as beds, tables, benches, stools are commonly employed. It seems also to have been common to set up tents, and other curtained and canopied spaces, on the stage itself, and to open and close them where necessary in the action.

*Fig. 3.* The Swan Theatre, London, *c.* 1596, as originally drawn by Johannes de Witt and copied by Arend van Buchell.

The only known contemporary drawing of an Elizabethan theatre, though still, in detail, much disputed.

The actors are all men or boys; the boys take the parts of women. There are certain conventional costumes, as for a Ghost, a Fool, and perhaps a Clown; masks, or vizors, are occasionally used; and there is, of course, armour for soldiers. But in the main, the dress of the actors is normal Elizabethan clothing, of as fine a quality as can be afforded.

The method of acting, although varying through the period, and in different kinds of play and scene, is in general conventional, in the sense that speech and action are clearly stylized and intensified from the speech and movements of ordinary life. The rhythms of verse and prose, and the various literary forms in which the words of the dramatic speech are arranged, are given their full quantity and emphasis; and this general method of delivery is closely accompanied by action, in the sense of certain formal movements and gestures, which are fitted to the movement of the language. It seems probable that these gestures and movements had been developed, by the professional actors, from the formal gestures of rhetoric, and given a new dramatic range.

Music is used in the performance, both for the accompaniment of songs, and in the general action. Instruments include trumpets, drums, viols, timbrels, bells, cornets, hautboys. A performance begins with three soundings of a trumpet; and approaches are frequently marked by 'flourishes' (of trumpets or cornets), and action indicated by 'alarums' (trumpets or drums). Other effects of sound, as of the firing of guns, or the thunder of a storm, are also available. Effects of light are occasionally used, although the performance is in full daylight: the carrying of torches, for instance, can be used to indicate an action at night.

For these conditions of performance, then, this play was written, and we must now look briefly at its text, before considering in detail parts of its actual performance.

## THE TEXT

*Antony and Cleopatra* is a play of 3,964 lines, in the First Folio text. In modern editions, it is divided into five acts, with a total of forty-two scenes, but these divisions do not indicate its original structure, and the separation of scenes, and even of acts, was not observed in the performance, in any way corresponding to contemporary act and scene divisions. The normal marking of acts and scenes, in modern texts of the play, is used here for convenience of reference; but the marking does not serve, indeed often hinders, perception of the play's actual progress. The text can be formally set out in the following way, to indicate the stages of the action:

*Act I, Scenes i–iii: Antony, Cleopatra and their attendants*

Antony and Cleopatra show their love; the general criticism of Antony's alliance with Cleopatra is realized; Antony receives messages of the death of his wife, Fulvia, and of the revolt of Pompey, and decides to return to Rome.

*Act I, Scene iv: Octavius Caesar, Lepidus and attendants*

Caesar receives news of Antony and Cleopatra at Alexandria, and of Pompey's strength. Caesar desires Antony's return.

*Act I, Scene v: Cleopatra, her women and Alexas*

Cleopatra thinks of her absent Antony, and receives a message from him.

*Act II, Scene i: Pompey and others*

Pompey, aware of Caesar's strength against him, is confident that Antony is still with Cleopatra, but receives news of his return to Rome.

*Act II, Scenes ii–iv: Antony, Caesar and their attendants*

Antony returns to Rome, and confirms his alliance with
Caesar, which is marked by his marriage to Caesar's sister
Octavia. Antony's stay with Cleopatra is recalled, and
Antony himself, in spite of his marriage, decides to return to
Cleopatra in Egypt.

*Act II, Scene v: Cleopatra, her women and a messenger*

Cleopatra receives news of Antony's marriage to Octavia.

*Act II, Scenes vi–vii: Antony, Caesar, Lepidus, Pompey and
attendants.*
The triumvirs (Antony, Caesar, Lepidus) meet Pompey and
reach an agreement with him, which they celebrate.

*Act III, Scene i: Ventidius and attendants*

Ventidius, Antony's officer, celebrates a victory over the
Parthians.

*Act III, Scene ii: Antony, Caesar, Lepidus, Octavia*

Caesar says farewell to Antony and Octavia, who are going
to Athens.

*Act III, Scene iii: Cleopatra, her women and a messenger*

Cleopatra is given a further account of Octavia.

*Act III, Scenes iv–v: Antony, Octavia, attendants*

Reports are given of Caesar's new wars on Pompey, of
Pompey's murder, and of Caesar's subjection of Lepidus. The
rivalry between Antony and Caesar again threatens, and
Octavia is its victim.

*Act III, Scene vi: Caesar, Octavia*

Octavia returns to Rome to her brother, and is told that
Antony has gone again to Egypt, to Cleopatra.

# Antony and Cleopatra, *by Shakespeare*

*Act III, Scene vii: Antony, Cleopatra, attendants*

Antony and Cleopatra prepare for the battle against Caesar.

*Act III, Scenes viii–x*

Antony and Caesar dispose their forces; the battle is fought, Cleopatra's ships break off, and Antony follows them.

*Act III, Scene xi: Antony, Cleopatra, attendants*

Cleopatra asks pardon for precipitating the defeat; Antony sees her as his conqueror.

*Act III, Scene xii: Caesar, attendants, Euphronius*

Antony's envoy, Euphronius, asks Caesar his terms. Antony asks that he may stay in Egypt, or else go to Athens. Caesar refuses, and orders Cleopatra to deliver up Antony.

*Act III, Scene xiii: Antony, Cleopatra, Thyreus, attendants*

Thyreus, Caesar's envoy, presents Caesar's terms to Cleopatra. Antony intervenes, and orders Thyreus to be whipped. He resolves to take the field again, and Cleopatra supports him.

*Act IV, Scene i: Caesar and attendants*

Caesar hears of Antony's defiance, and pities him. Many of Antony's troops have now deserted to Caesar.

*Act IV, Scene ii: Antony, Cleopatra, attendants*

Antony and Cleopatra prepare a feast, on the night before the final battle.

*Act IV, Scene iii: Antony's soldiers*

The guard in Antony's camp hears strange music, which is taken as an omen.

*Act IV, Scenes iv–v: Antony, Cleopatra, Eros, attendants*

Antony arms, and goes out with his lieutenant, Eros.

*Act IV, Scene vi: Caesar, Agrippa, Enobarbus*

Caesar orders Agrippa to take Antony alive. Enobarbus, who has deserted from Antony, finds that Antony has sent his treasure after him, and resolves to die in his shame.

*Act IV, Scene vii: Agrippa, Antony, attendants*

In the fighting, Caesar's forces are beaten back.

*Act IV, Scene viii: Antony, Cleopatra, attendants*

Antony marches back in victory, and he and Cleopatra prepare to re-enter Alexandria in triumph.

*Act IV, Scene ix: Caesar's soldiers, Enobarbus*

Enobarbus kills himself in Caesar's camp.

*Act IV, Scenes x–xii: Antony, Caesar, soldiers*

The next day's battle is prepared, and fought, at sea. Antony's fleet deserts to Caesar. Antony blames Cleopatra for treachery.

*Act IV, Scene xiii: Cleopatra, her women, Mardian*

Cleopatra, in fear of Antony, sends Mardian to tell him that she is dead.

*Act IV, Scene xiv: Antony, Eros, Mardian*

Antony is given the feigning news of Cleopatra's death, and resolves to die himself. He asks Eros to kill him, but Eros turns the sword on himself. Antony falls on his sword, but is only wounded. A new messenger comes from Cleopatra, taking back the false report of her death. Antony calls his guard to carry him to Cleopatra.

*Act IV, Scene xv: Antony, Cleopatra, attendants*

Antony is drawn up into the monument where Cleopatra hides from Caesar, and dies in her presence.

# Antony and Cleopatra, *by Shakespeare*

*Act V, Scene i: Caesar and his adjutants*

Caesar receives the sword of Antony, with news of his death. He send Proculeius to Cleopatra.

*Act V, Scene ii: Cleopatra, her women, Proculeius, Caesar, etc.*

Cleopatra is seized in her monument, but Proculeius assures her of Caesar's bounty. Caesar visits her, and she pretends to acknowledge him. But she has procured a Clown to bring her asps, and she and her servant die by them. Caesar returns to find Cleopatra dead, and orders that she 'shall be buried by her Antony'. Then, away to Rome.

A summary of this kind is no more than a brief and abstract chronicle. In this play, where the essential action is in the poetry, there can be no ordinary summary. But the form allows us to see the logic of the general action. The dominant element is movement, rather than a simple, isolable pattern. The action ranges in space over half the Mediterranean, and has been calculated, in historic time, as covering ten years. But these considerations are wholly external. Space is an element in the play, emphasizing its magnitude, but the primary agent of this is the acted speech, the spoken action, which is the vital pattern. The action which Shakespeare creates, and which his stage could so readily perform, is a movement governed by the tragic experience. The rapid and varied succession of scenes is a true sequence; we shall wholly misunderstand it if we separate the scenes, and think of them as making their effect singly. The construction of the play has often been condemned, on the grounds of its frequent shifts and apparent disintegration. But this is to look for integration in the wrong place: in the realistic representation of time and place which have little to do with this kind of drama. The measure of time in the play is the dramatic verse; the reality of place is the reality of played action on the stage.

The dramatic integration – like the movement employed to realize it – rests in the structure of feeling which the dramatic verse, as a whole organization, communicates. This structure of feeling is the essential reality which the text embodies, and which the performance will manifest.

## Act I, Scene i

The trumpet has sounded for the beginning of the performance and two friends of Antony, Philo and Demetrius, come forward over the empty stage. Philo speaks:

> Nay, but this dotage of our Generals
> Ore-flowes the measure: those his goodly eyes
> That o're the Files and Musters of the Warre,
> Have glow'd like plated Mars:
> Now bend, now turne
> The Office and Devotion of their view
> Upon a Tawny Front. His Captaines heart,
> Which in the scuffles of great Fights hath burst
> The Buckles on his brest, reneages all temper,
> And is become the Bellowes and the Fan
> To coole a Gypsies Lust.

What we notice about this speech is not only that we are being moved at once into the heart of the action (although the speed and clarity are admirable), but also that an essential element in the total structure of feeling is being, not reported, but enacted. That is to say, Philo's speech is not just a narrative to introduce us to Antony; the very form of the speech enacts an essential movement of the play. The two placing phrases are *ore-flowes the measure* and *reneages all temper*; and between these, the construction of the words, in figure and rhythm, performs the particular movement. Thus,

those his goodly eyes
That o're the Files and Musters of the Warre,
Have glow'd like plated Mars:

creates Antony, the warrior chief, who is then set immediately
in antithesis with the doting general: not by report, but by the
rhythm (the Folio punctuation allows us to see this clearly,
where the punctuation of a modern edition obscures; compare

Have glow'd like plated Mars, now bend, now turn

with

Have glow'd like plated Mars:
Now bend, now turne)

and by the figure: the eyes that *glow'd* now *bend*. And both the
rhythm and the figure are consciously emphasized in performance; not only the voice pointing the rhythm, but also
the hands creating the antithesis, and the movement of the
head, the expression of the face, enacting the change from the
*goodly eyes/That o're the Files and Musters of the Warre/Have
glow'd* to the *now bend, now turne ... Upon a Tawny Front.*

At once, indeed, in this performance which the writing
makes necessary, we find the creation, not only of a dramatic
situation, but of a dramatic rhythm; and this is not only
audible, it is also visible. And now, immediately, the trumpets
sound a flourish, and Antony and Cleopatra enter, in formal
train, and attended. The emphasis of *a Gypsies Lust* still sounds
in our ears with the trumpets, and the important tension of
the play is at once set. The cheapening phrase, and the quickening state, are set at once in opposition. As the train advances
down stage, we hear again Philo's words:

Looke where they come:
Take but good note, and you shall see in him

(The triple Pillar of the world) transform'd
Into a Strumpets Foole. Behold and see.

The strength of the original emotion is powerfully reinforced, but we are looking now at *the triple Pillar of the world*,
and at the *strumpet*: they have taken the centre of the stage,
and Philo and Demetrius are merely watchers. The opposing
element, first evident in the magnificence of the entry, is now
again stressed in the formal verse which Antony and Cleopatra
speak.

c.: If it be Love indeed, tell me how much.
a.: There's beggery in the love that can be reckon'd.
c.: Ile set a bourne how farre to be belov'd.
a.: Then must thou needes finde out new Heaven,
    new Earth.

This is not ordinary dramatic dialogue, of an establishing
kind, any more than Philo's speech was an introductory
report. The question and answer, the balancing single lines,
are as formal as song, and in performance are given their full
emphasis: a momentarily isolated pattern that creates a whole
feeling. It is, in a sense a deliberate emphasis of stillness, and
in its beauty is very different from the picture for which Philo
had prepared us. We were prepared for baseness, and we see
magnificence; and both emotions are important. For in fact
the figures interact, in their own tension: the magnificence of
*needes finde out new Heaven, new Earth* – the breaking of all
bounds for love – is an echo, in a different way, of *ore-flowes
all measure*, where the *love* was *dotage*. And it is just this movement, this interaction, which is a principal movement of the
play as a whole: now set before us, in words and action, in the
first nineteen lines.

In a Shakespearean play of this kind, the dramatic rhythm –
the whole movement of the play, as communicated in acted

speech – is always both definite and complex. For now, immediately, there is a new break, and a change. A Messenger enters, and as we still hear Antony's *new Heaven, new Earth, Newes (my good Lord) from Rome* come the messenger's words. The transition is pointed by the emphasis of *Newes*, and the name of *Rome*, the particular place, is set against the imagined *new Heaven, new Earth*. And then the break is marked by the staccato of Antony's reply:

> Grates me, the summe.

In performance, the break in the verbal music is similarly marked; compare *Ile set a bourne how farre to be belov'd* with *Grates, me the summe*. And now Cleopatra, too, speaks in quite a different way:

> Nay heare them Anthony.
> Fulvia perchance is angry: Or who knowes,
> If the scarse-bearded Caesar have not sent
> His powrefull Mandate to you. Do this, or this;
> Take in that Kingdome, and Infranchise that:
> Perform't, or else we damne thee.

The words are bitter in Cleopatra's right, but in performance the speech creates not only Cleopatra, but the *powrefull Mandate* of *scarse-bearded Caesar*: the orders are played as orders with the quick gestures of command. Cleopatra continues the taunt, but Antony, when he comes to reply, returns deliberately to the former rhythms. The contrast is again deliberate, and pointed:

> c.: ... When shrill-tongu'd Fulvia scolds. The Messengers.
> a.: Let Rome in Tyber melt, and the wide Arch
>   Of the raing'd Empire fall: Heere is my space,
>   Kingdomes are clay: Our dungie earth alike
>   Feeds Beast as Man: the Noblenesse of life
>   Is to do thus: when such a mutuall paire,

And such a twaine can doo't, in which I binde
On paine of punishment, the world to weete
We stand up Peerelesse.

The acted speech, here, is an intense creation of the towering
scale of the drama: of the willing contemplation of ruin, that
again *ore-flowes all measure*, and of the equal magnificence of
the attachment: *Heere is my space*. It is significant that it is at
once followed again by the discordance, in Cleopatra's:

Excellent falshood:
Why did he marry Fulvia, and not love her?
Ile seeme the Foole I am not. Anthony will be himselfe.

And the method of this speech underlines the nature of the
action. The scene is not merely dialogue – the actors of Antony
and Cleopatra standing and talking *to* one another; it is,
rather, a *presentation*, and Cleopatra, in speaking of Antony as
*he*, is not to be supposed to be talking aside (as modern editors
indicate). The manner of Elizabethan performance, in which
the actors are acting dramatic verse to an audience, rather than
representing behaviour, allows a variation of this kind,
without embarrassment. Cleopatra widens the terms of
reference by the greater distancing of her speech; but her
words are presented to the audience, in the same way as
Antony's great invocation is presented. Neither is what we
know from modern drama as acted conversation.

One final point may be noted about this scene. We have
seen how, through the formal arrangement and contrast of
the verse, a complex pattern of feeling has been clearly
enacted. The verse has enforced this pattern, but there is also
something else, which in reading the scene may not be realized
but in Elizabethan performance is clear. This is the necessary
magnificence of both Antony and Cleopatra, as they appear
to us: a magnificence against which the elements of ruin and

of baseness are set in the necessary tension which is the dramatic movement of the whole play. There is no doubt that in performance this magnificence is constant, even while the other conflicting elements sound. We see its text in Antony's words to Cleopatra:

> Fye wrangling Queene:
> Whom every thing becomes, to chide, to laugh,
> To weepe; who every passion fully strives
> To make it selfe (in Thee) faire, and admir'd.

It is what is later said of her, by Enobarbus, after the long invocation of her magnificence on Cydnus:

> . . . she did make defect, perfection
> . . . For vildest things
> Become themselves in her, that the holy Priests
> Blesse her, when she is Riggish.

And it is this, in performance, that is necessarily enacted, in a way that can be seen in the deliberate contrast with Octavia. Antony says of Octavia:

> Her tongue will not obey her heart, nor can
> Her heart informe her tongue;

and the Messenger says of her, to Cleopatra's question:

c.: What Majestie is in her gate, remember,
  If ere thou look'st on Majestie.
m.: She creepes: her motion, and her station are as one:
  She shewes a body, rather then a life,
  A Statue, then a Breather.

This is not (as it may now read) merely reported characterization, but would be enacted in performance. The boy actors playing the two women would, in all their movements, enforce the contrast: the magnificent Cleopatra, *who every*

*passion fully strives to make it selfe (in Thee) faire, and admir'd*;
and the restraint of Octavia, whose heart will not *inform her
tongue*, whose *motion* and *station* (movement and standing) are
as one. The contrast of movement is clear, but it is not
movement alone, but part of the acted speech. The poetry of
Cleopatra is not an irrelevant general beauty, but the heart
informing the tongue, so that voice and movement, the
whole body of the speech, enacts decisively one *whom every
thing becomes*. The consummation of her speech before death –

> I am Fire, and Ayre; my other Elements
> I give to baser life

– rests dramatically on the whole *becoming* that we have seen
throughout the play. And just as this is set against the external
judgement of *strumpet*, so is the whole body of the acted speech
of Antony set against the similar judgement of *strumpet's foole*.
I do not mean that these judgements are irrelevant; they are,
rather, insisted upon, in order to create the actual dramatic
tension between the judgement and the attachment. What is
said of Antony interacts with the Antony we see and hear –
*his rear'd arme crested the world*. For characterization, in this
kind of drama, has the strength of the whole dramatic verse,
enacted at its own level. It is not merely report, but performance,

> ... when such a mutuall paire,
> We stand up peerelesse.

This magnificence is actual, and all the modes of performance
– language, movement, gesture and appearance – combine
to present it. It is as Cleopatra says to Antony:

> Eternity was in our Lippes, and Eyes,
> Blisse in our browes bent: none our parts so poore,
> But was a race of Heaven. They are so still ...

Shakespeare wrote his dramatic verse, not to decorate a situation, but to be able to create, in a variety of modes, effects of this kind. The persons are not so much represented in behaviour, as created in performance, through the intensity of the dramatic rhythm, which the text exactly prescribes, and which the performance communicates, in a single embodiment of voice and movement. We do not see, in fact,

> Some squeaking Cleopatra Boy my greatnesse
> I' th' posture of a Whore.

Shakespeare could not have written this, making a deliberate contrast of effect, had he not known that the performed drama – the dramatic rhythm enacted, as it were impersonally, by every means of intensity in voice and movement – would enforce something very different: the *strong toyle of Grace* which is here, ultimately, beyond persons, but which an artist could imagine, and write, and which his performers, through the deliberate arts of speech and movement, could embody. *Heere is my space*, indeed; not Alexandria, nor the years of that dynasty, but this stage, where such an action can be performed.

## Act IV, Scene III

We can turn now, briefly, to a scene of a different kind, which illustrates another aspect of Elizabethan performance. It is marked in modern editions as Act IV, Scene iii, and shows a company of Antony's soldiers, on the night before the second battle. The stage is empty for a moment, and then the soldiers enter:

1 SOL.: Brother, goodnight: to morrow is the day.
2 SOL.: It will determine one way: Fare you well.
    Heard you of nothing strange about the streets?
1 SOL.: Nothing: what newes?
2 SOL.: Belike 'tis but a Rumour, good night to you.
1 SOL.: Well sir, good night.

Already we hear in these words a curious premonitory rhythm, which is emphasized when in performance they are spoken in a deliberate pattern, and not as isolated separate remarks. The soldiers move across the stage, bearing torches to create the night watch (we have just heard Antony's words:

> I . . . did desire you
> To burne this night with Torches)

and now they meet other soldiers, and again the speech is formal:

> 2 SOL.: Souldiers, have carefull Watch.
> 1 SOL.: And you: Goodnight, goodnight.

And now, interestingly, the performance direction is that *they place themselves in every corner of the stage*. The whole playing space, with the soldiers standing disposed in their watch, is occupied. The formal speech continues, in its marked rhythm:

> 2 SOL.: Heere we: and if to morrow
> Our Navie thrive, I have an absolute hope
> Our Landmen will stand up.
> 1 SOL.: 'Tis a brave Army, and full of purpose.

And now, suddenly, as they stand, *musicke of the Hoboyes is under the Stage*. (The *hoboyes* are not one instrument, but a family, including treble, alto, tenor and bass types, regularly played as a 'band'.)

> 2: Peace, what noise?
> 1: List list.
> 2: Hearke.
> 1: Musicke i' th' Ayre.
> 3: Under the earth.
> 4: It signes well, do's it not?
> 3: No.
> 1: Peace I say: What should this meane?

2: 'Tis the God Hercules, whom Anthony loved
  Now leaves him.

The haunting effect of the unseen music is taken into a deliberate pattern with the speech and movement of the soldiers, who
are acting indeed, here, as a kind of chorus:

1: Walke, let's see if other Watchmen
  Do heare what we do?
2: How now Maisters?

And now the soldiers speak all together:

OMNES: How now? how now? do you heare this?
1: I, is't not strange?
3: Do you heare Masters? Do you heare?
1: Follow the noyse so farre as we have quarter.
  Let's see how it will give off.
OMNES: Content: 'Tis strange.

And so with the music still playing, and as it were moving
away, they move together, in its train, and leave the stage.
They take their torches with them, leaving the stage empty,
and when, a moment later, Antony and Cleopatra enter, it is
morning, and Antony will arm.

The dramatic method of the scene need hardly be stressed.
It creates directly, through the verse, the movement, and the
music, a clear pattern both of night and of omen.

### The Deaths of Antony and Cleopatra

We can look now at a later part of the action, in which we
see, not only the dramatic fullness of the acted verse, but also a
particular use of the Elizabethan stage. Eros is with Antony
after his final defeat, and they are standing together at the
front of the stage. Antony has spoken of the images of the
clouds, that

> mocke our eyes with Ayre.
> Thou hast seene these Signes,
> They are blacke Vespers Pageants . . .
> That which is now a Horse, even with a thoght
> The Racke dislimes, and makes it indistinct
> As water is in water . . .
> My good Knave Eros, now thy Captaine is
> Even such a body.

And now Mardian enters, and brings the false report of Cleopatra's death. Antony tells Eros that he knows he himself must
now die. He will not be taken and humiliated by Caesar;
and now, suddenly, the humiliation is for an instant present,
not by report, or thought, but in the acted speech:

> Eros,
> Would'st thou be window'd in great Rome, and see
> Thy Master thus with pleacht Armes, bending downe
> His corrigible necke, his face subdu'de
> To penetrative shame . . .

The flexibility of the dramatic method is nowhere more
apparent: for just as, in the general body of Antony's speech,
his greatness is manifested in the whole power of words and
movement, here, by assuming the formal posture of defeat
and humiliation, the emotion is not narrative, or imagination,
but an actual dramatic presence, in the *pleacht armes, bending
downe his . . . necke, his face subdu'de*. The conventional for-
mality of this posture is of the same kind, dramatically, as the
normal evidence of his greatness: so that the tension between
greatness and defeat is fully and visibly enacted. And Antony
remains thus bowed, asking Eros to kill him. But Eros turns
the sword on himself, and Antony is forced to recover his own
greatness. Here again, the movement is wholly dramatic, as
Antony lifts his head, unfolds his arms, and, looking up, can
act again for himself:

Antony and Cleopatra, *by Shakespeare*

> My Queene and Eros
> Have by their brave instruction got upon me
> A Noblenesse in Record. But I will bee
> A Bride-groome in my death, and run intoo't
> As to a Lovers bed.

He runs himself on his own sword, but the wound is not immediately fatal. He calls the guard, and asks them to make an end of him. Here, once again, as when the soldiers heard the music, there is a brief and formal choral pattern:

> 2 SOL.: The Starre is falne.
> 1 SOL.: And time is at his Period.
> ALL: Alas, and woe.
> ANT.: Let him that loves me, strike me dead.
> 1 SOL.: Not I.
> 2 SOL.: Nor I.
> 3 SOL.: Nor any one.

And as Antony is left dying, news comes that Cleopatra still lives. He calls his guard again, and asks to be carried to Cleopatra:

> Take me up,
> I have led you oft, carry me now good Friends,
> And have my thankes for all.

Five of his guards raise him, and bear him slowly off the stage. As they disappear, Cleopatra, with Charmian and Iras, and her maids, enters *aloft*.

It is one of the major difficulties, in imagining an Elizabethan or early Jacobean performance, to know how to take this 'aloft', which is a quite common direction. There are advantages in taking it as the gallery, which is a permanent structure, and for simple scenes, as in an address from the town walls or battlements, it is undoubtedly the best choice. But when, as now, a substantial scene is to be played there, the gallery, behind its balustrade, is badly placed and restricted. The only alternative, however, is the curtained frame or scaffold, called variously 'tent' and 'mansion', for which there is good but not wholly convincing evidence. If we accept this device, set against the back wall, its interior is available for scenes of discovery, by the drawing of curtains (what used to be imagined as the 'inner stage', under the gallery, for which there is no strong evidence), and its roof for entrances 'aloft', when a substantial scene is to be played. Given the flexibility of this theatre, a scene can begin in a restricted space and move outwards, in playing, to occupy the main stage, and it is just this necessary movement which is the strongest argument against a gallery, for a scene of any major dramatic importance. At the same time, it is only by inference that we can imagine a 'tent' or 'mansion' roofed strongly enough for six or seven people to play a scene on it, as in *Antony and Cleopatra* they must now do. There is also the problem of where it comes from, if it is to be this substantial. There is evidence of a 'throne' or 'canopy' being lowered on to the stage, from the place where it normally hung, and some scholars have imagined it being brought on by scene-shifters. If the 'tent' is indeed, here, to be Cleopatra's monument – and its advantages over the gallery are in many ways obvious – it seems probable that it has been there throughout the play, and perhaps often associated with Cleopatra: there is an obvious use for its interior at the beginning of Act IV, Scene iv, and several similar possible uses. On one theory, indeed, the 'tent' or 'pavilion' would be regularly set up on the platform stage, against the rear curtained wall, for almost all performances.

However this detail may be settled, we have, as the physical playing area, two levels, and the scene is written with an awareness and a use of this dramatic relationship. Cleopatra and her attendants enter on the upper level:

CLEO: How now? is he dead?

DIOM.: His death's upon him, but not dead.
  Looke out o'th other side your Monument,
  His Guard have brought him thither.

Diomedes is on the lower level of the main stage. He directs
Cleopatra to look out on the other side, as Antony is carried in.
She moves to see him.

CLEO.: Oh Sunne,
  Burne the great Sphere thou mov'st in, darkling stand
  The varrying shore o' th' world. O Antony, Antony,
  Antony
  Helpe Charmian, helpe Iras helpe: helpe Friends
  Below, let's draw him hither.

These two that we have seen so often together are now
separated by this evident physical distance: the gap between
the two levels. They speak, at this distance, and then Cleopatra
cries again:

      ... but come, come Anthony,
      Helpe me my women, we must draw thee up:
      Assist good Friends.

With the guard supporting Antony from below, Cleopatra,
and her five attendants, prepare to draw him up. The writing
of this physical action is very interesting:

CLEO.: Heere's sport indeede:
  How heavy weighes my Lord?
  Our strength is all gone into heavinesse,
  That makes the waight. Had I great Iuno's power,
  The strong wing'd Mercury should fetch thee up,
  And set thee by Iove's side. Yet come a little,
  Wishers were ever fooles. Oh come, come, come,
  And welcome, welcome. Dye where thou hast lived,

Quicken with kissing: had my lippes that power,
Thus would I weare them out.

There are five guards below, who raise Antony until he is up
on their extended arms: this would be already between six
and seven feet above the stage. And then, on the upper level,
there are Cleopatra, Iras, Charmian, Diomedes and at least
two maids: six persons to receive him. There could be a use
of ropes, for which there is some evidence in similar cases,
but the movement could also be carried out by the use of arms
alone; there are eleven people to lift and receive one. And the
process of the lift is used as an explicit dramatic element in the
verse:

> Our strength is all gone into heavinesse,
> That makes the waight.

The powerful, strong-standing Antony, whom we have seen
throughout, is now an inert, almost dead, weight. But see the
quickening as Cleopatra at last touches and receives him:

> Oh come, come, come . . .

and the echo of this as he is finally in her arms:

> And welcome, welcome.

As he lies in her arms, she kisses him, while the attendants
above and below watch, concentrated on the two figures. Then
Antony comes to his last words:

> The miserable change now at my end,
> Lament nor sorrow at: but please your thoughts
> In feeding them with those my former Fortunes
> Wherein I lived. The greatest Prince o' th' world,
> The Noblest: and do now not basely dye,
> Not Cowardly put off my helmet to
> My Countreyman. A Roman, by a Roman

> Valiantly vanquish'd. Now my Spirit is going,
>     I can no more.

He sinks from Cleopatra's arms, but the note is struck – not merely the note of Antony, but of the whole movement:

> The Noblest: and do now not basely dye.

Cleopatra takes up the word, and raises the pattern to its peak of intensity:

> Noblest of men, woo't dye?
> Hast thou no care of me, shall I abide
> In this dull world, which in thy absence is
> No better than a Stye? Oh see my women:
> The Crowne o' th' Earth doth melt. My Lord?
> Oh wither'd is the Garland of the Warre,
> The Souldiers pole is falne; young Boyes and Gyrles
> Are levell now with men: The oddes is gone,
> And there is nothing left remarkeable
> Beneath the visiting Moone.

This supreme dramatic verse creates its own music of action, but while it flares into this intensity of the voice, the physical situation continues to support it. The guards still stand below; the women are grouped above. Antony has fallen, and we are intensely aware of the levels as we watch. The ideas are taken into the verse, and are transformed; but all, at this moment, are part of a single situation.

Now Cleopatra, too, has fallen across the body of Antony, and Charmian and Iras fear that she is dead, and call on her. Once again it is the magnificence that is emphasized: *Lady . . . Soveraigne . . . Lady . . . Madam . . . Oh Madam, Madam, Madam . . . Royall Egypt: Empresse.* And Cleopatra rises again, and looks round on her women, and on the guards below:

> My noble Gyrles? Ah Women, women! Looke
> Our Lampe is spent, it's out. Good sirs, take heart,

Wee'l bury him: And then, what's brave, what's Noble,
Let's doo't after the high Roman fashion,
And make death proud to take us. Come, away,
This case of that huge Spirit now is cold.
Ah Women, Women! Come, we have no Friend
But Resolution, and the breefest end.

The emphatic, conclusive rhyme ends the scene; and the guards
below go out, while, above, Antony's body is carried away.

The whole stage is then empty, but is at once occupied by
Caesar. Antony's bloodstained sword is brought to him, and
he will go to Cleopatra. The flexibility of this stage is then
again remarkably demonstrated. There is the physical occupa-
tion by Caesar, and then a return to Cleopatra, on the upper
level. Caesar's messenger comes to her, and they speak from
different levels. But then:

GALLUS: You see how easily she may be surprised.
Guard her till Caesar come.

There are no directions in the original text. Cleopatra is seized,
by a sudden movement and entry, and after her lament –

Shall they hoist me up
And show me to the shouting varletry
Of censuring Rome?

Dolabella comes and takes her, guarded, from Proculeius.
It is in her capture, and in being passed from hand to hand,
that she is brought down to the main stage level, where Caesar
will come, with his train, and where she will kneel to him.
After her apparent submission, it is here, moving to the front
of the stage, that she makes her own climax.

Give me my Robe, put on my Crowne, I have
Immortall longings in me. Now no more

Antony and Cleopatra, *by Shakespeare*

The juyce of Egypts Grape shall moyst this lip.
Yare, yare, good Iras; quicke.

The intense speech, in this climax, is supported at every point
by movement and design; or rather, it is speech in which
dramatic movement and design are inherent.

From this assertion of her royalty, Cleopatra turns to the
sleep of death. She moves back to the curtained bed, where,
as she takes the asp:

>Peace, peace:
>Dost thou not see my Baby at my breast
>That suckes the Nurse asleepe.

The writing and the acting are parts of a single dramatic
image. The scene moves to a kind of sleep:

>Downy windows close
>And golden Phoebus never be beheld
>Of eyes again so royall. Your crown's awry
>I'll mend it, and then play.

This is Charmian arranging the state of the dead queen,
withdrawn but visible. It leaves the main area of the stage
again open for the return of Caesar and his train. As they
discover the deaths, the dramatic intensity returns, in another
voice, that of Caesar:

>She looks like sleep
>As she would catch another Anthony
>In her strong toyle of grace.

This, again, is not only a metaphor; it is a written and visible
dramatic image. It is from here that Caesar must move her:

>Take up her bed
>And bear her women from the monument.

He salutes the memory of Antony and Cleopatra, and the procession bearing the dead –

> High order in this great solemnity

– moves across and away, leaving the stage empty.

# 5

## Plays in Transition

WE can next look at some instances of that long and complicated development of plays and theatres, from the greatness of
Elizabethan drama to the remarkable revival of European
drama in the late nineteenth and twentieth centuries. We
shall see parts of three plays in performance: William Wycherley's *The Plain Dealer* (1676); George Lillo's *The London
Merchant* (1731); and Tom Robertson's *Caste* (1867). We shall
also look at what happened to a particular kind of dramatic
action, by a comparison of scenes in Shakespeare's *Hamlet*
and Ibsen's *The Feast of Solhoug*.

### *The Plain Dealer* by William Wycherley; 1676

#### THE CONDITIONS OF PERFORMANCE

*The Plain Dealer* was first produced at the Theatre Royal,
Drury Lane, on 11 December 1676. It was performed again
two nights later. Much had altered, in the English theatre,
since the performance of *Antony and Cleopatra*. The public
theatres had been closed, during the period of the Civil War
and the Commonwealth, between 1642 and 1660. When
they were reopened, there were some critical changes: they
were fewer in number; their audiences were greatly restricted,
being largely confined to the court and people associated
with it; and actresses came to join the previously all-male
companies. At the time of the production of *The Plain Dealer*,
there were in effect only two theatres in London; and this

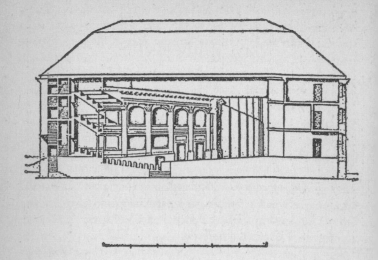

*Fig. 4.* Section of a theatre, probably Drury Lane. From a design by Sir Christopher Wren.

one, the Theatre Royal in Drury Lane, had been newly built in the last four years.

If we look at this theatre in section, we see that the depth of the stage is approximately equal to the depth of the auditorium, as it had been in the Elizabethan playhouses. But the stage no longer projects into the pit, and the audience no longer surrounds it on three sides. The spectators, nevertheless, come up to the front of the stage, and in some cases on to it. At a point midway in the depth of the stage, there is now a proscenium arch, and in the area behind it – the 'house' – there are wings and flats of painted scenery. The playing area can be entered through these, and scenes can be drawn to discover actors behind them. Most entrances, however, are made in front of the proscenium arch, where there are two doors on each side, and above them boxes, continuing the line of the gallery but in the case of those over the stage available for the action. The greater part of the performance takes place on this stage in front of the proscenium arch, and the curtain in the arch is only occasionally drawn.

## THE TEXT

Most Restoration plays, and certainly all its comedies, are radically affected by the special relationship between the limited theatre companies and the small, fashionable audience. There were many complaints that the theatres were used primarily for people in this circle to meet their friends, on an afternoon in a crowded, ingrown social life, and that it was sometimes difficult for the company to get a hearing above the talk. On the other hand, when, as in *The Plain Dealer*, just this talk and this life were the material of the play, there was an unusually close relationship between play and audience, and correspondingly between text and performance. The play was written by a man who was often in that audience, for a particular company (under the King's patronage, and the King was present at this first performance of *The Plain Dealer*) and a particular theatre.

The central convention of *The Plain Dealer* is indeed just the talk of this limited world. It is a critical replaying of these styles and manners. The sea-captain, Manly, returned from the Dutch wars, despises the flattery and gossip of the town, and makes his way through a series of encounters which confirm his contempt for it. What ought to ruin him, in his plain dealing, is, all the same, redeemed: he is followed everywhere by a girl dressed in man's clothes, who secretly and honestly loves him, and who has the advantage of being an heiress. There is thus a combination of plain dealing, in the

substance and manner of the play, with a romantic convention which permits the hero's improbable triumph.


PERFORMANCE

We can look, briefly, at the Prologue and at one critical
Act. The prologue is spoken by the Plain Dealer himself,
with an edge which, in its direct challenge to the behaviour
of the audience –

> Now, you shrewd judges, who the boxes sway
> Leading the ladies' hearts and sense astray,
> And, for their sakes, see all, and hear no play –
> Correct your cravats, foretops, look behind;
> The dress and breeding of the play ne'er mind;
> Plain dealing is, you'll say, quite out of fashion

– anticipates the character's challenge, in a rougher idiom,
to that similar world as reflected on the stage. This linking
of action and audience, as in a mirror effect, makes for an
immediate force and consistency of style. Only at the end is
the line between audience and action drawn, and then in the
same critical mood:

> And where else but on stages do we see
> Truth pleasing, or rewarded honesty?
> Which our bold poet does today in me?
> If not to the honest, be to th' prosp'rous kind:
> Some friends at court let the Plain Dealer find.

As the play is launched, on an unseparated, uncurtained stage,
the action is dominated by this sardonic voice, which produces, as it were, a series of scenes which are the target for
just such a commentary. Manly's tirades, directed at once
inward to the stage and outward to the audience, are the
points around which the whole play is organized.

For more detail of the performance, we may look, generally, at Act Three. In the 'house' behind the proscenium arch there is a painted backcloth of Westminster Hall. This has on it, within the architecture, several painted figures, who are the crowded background. The Act is then a series of rapid encounters – in effect, a kind of procession with commentary – in which the business and manners of the town, here around a law-court, are openly and flexibly displayed. Manly enters with Freeman and two sailors through one of the doors at the front, and looks through to the scene of the Hall, under which are a group of gowned lawyers (*at the end of the stage*). While Freeman goes to them, Manly turns to the audience, and speaks directly:

> How hard it is to be a hypocrite!
> At least to me, who am but newly so ...

Fidelia, disguised as a young man, comes in to him at the front of the stage; he gives her a commission to the woman he still wants to trust, Olivia. (In the immediately preceding scene, with the same effect of a display with commentary, we have seen Olivia cheating with Novel and Plausible, in what is established as a room, with its doors and windows opening on to the stage, but where, at the same time, Manly and Freeman can enter and *stand behind*, overhearing but unobserved. For all the greater detail of scenery, the flexibility of place of the Elizabethan stage is still assumed as a convention. So, also, is another convention, of a kind of open disguise, though now with an actress dressed as a young man.) Fidelia, when Manly in his turn has gone to *the end of the stage*, in the direction of the hall where the background crowd is still present, turns alone to the audience and speaks of her own situation.

The essential dramatic relations of the performance are then evident. What is being continually shown is the crowded movement of this London life, as a background out of which particular figures emerge to describe and disclose themselves, ultimately in relation to the as yet isolated figures of Manly and Fidelia, who can speak their own feelings directly to the audience. This rapid and complicated movement is brilliantly maintained. Thus, when Fidelia leaves, the Widow Blackacre comes on

[*in the middle of half a dozen lawyers, whispered to by a fellow in black;* JERRY BLACKACRE *following the crowd.*]

Figures detach themselves – Serjeant Ploddon, Lawyer Quaint, Petulant – and merge again – in the whirl and calculation of pleadings and plans. Another lawyer, Buttongown, crosses the stage *in haste*, but is pursued and caught by the Widow Blackacre, and then gets away again. Major Oldfox and the Bookseller's Boy pass through, in the same rush of calculation and selling. While Widow Blackacre is talking to them, again

[*Several cross the stage.*]

and she is in a new pursuit of What-d'ye-call-him. The rush continues, between Manly, Oldfox, the two Blackacres. Each, at every point, is using and calculating in the complicated business, except for Manly, who is pointing what they are doing. As the rush of the town continues a lawyer and then an alderman hurry through, stopping only to be, as it were, interviewed by Manly. The emphasis is consistent:

ALDERMAN: Business, sir, I say, must be done.

[*Several crossing the stage.*]

ALDERMAN: And there's an officer of the treasury I have an affair with.

[*Exit* ALDERMAN.]

Manly, left alone with Freeman at the front of the stage, while the rush continues behind them, draws the experience together:

MANLY: You see now what the mighty friendship of the world is; what all ceremony, embraces, and plentiful professions come to: you are no more to believe a profess-ing friend than a threat'ning enemy; and as no man hurts you, that tells you he'll do you a mischief, no man, you see, is your servant, who says he is so.

And then finally, turning to the still crowded stage behind him, with its painted backcloth – the real figures merging with the painted figures – Freeman makes a last point:

FREEMAN: Three or four hundred years ago, a man might have dined in this hall.

They go out, with Manly speaking a rhyming sentence, and what has been articulated, as a description of the world, has also, in a unity of writing and performance, been passing, as if in a kaleidoscope, in front of us.

## *The London Merchant* by George Lillo: 1731

### THE CONDITIONS OF PERFORMANCE

Fifty-five years later, in the same theatre of Drury Lane, Lillo's *The London Merchant* entered the English repertory in which it was to be a regular item for the next hundred years, after its first performance on 22 June 1731. There is some important continuity between Wycherley's theatre and Lillo's, but there are also some changes. Part of the stage in front of the proscenium arch has been cut off, to make more room for the benches in the pit, and there are now only two entrance doors, and their corresponding gallery boxes, level with the front of the stage. The audience still comes up close to the stage, and is still often noisy; there are many stories of riots and fights in the theatres. There is no longer the intimate connection between the audience and the court, but this is still a fashionable world, now expanding and including many more successful middle-class people. There are more theatres, and in the rush of shows, entertainments and gaming the drama itself is very mixed in kind and quality.

### THE TEXT

*The London Merchant* made its way in this period of intense activity and display. Its emphasis is given in its prologue:

> The Tragic Muse, sublime, delights to show
> Princes distrest and scenes of royal woe
>
> ... Forgive us then, if we attempt to show,
> In artless strains, a tale of private woe.
> A London 'prentice ruined, is our theme.

Though nominally set, following an old ballad, in 1587, the play dramatizes, in a self-conscious way, a moral tale for the times. George Barnwell, the apprentice, is seduced from his master Thorowgood's interest by Mistress Millwood, and is led on to theft and murder. His companion apprentice, Trueman, stays with Thorowgood, marries his daughter, and is present at the end to see Barnwell and Millwood hanged, with a properly self-conscious and moralizing distress:

> In vain
> With bleeding hearts and weeping eyes we show
> A human, gen'rous sense of others' woe,
> Unless we mark what drew their ruin on,
> And, by avoiding that – prevent our own.

These are the formally defining verses. The body of the play is in prose, but this is not now the direct and vigorous local idiom of Wycherley, but a self-conscious theatrical prose, projecting and describing sentiments. The writing and the performance have this common quality, as we can see by looking at the final act.

## Act Five

The stage is empty, and then a painted backcloth is drawn, just behind the proscenium arch. We are in a room in a prison. This method of establishing place is now more frequently used than in the Restoration drama: similar painted scenes, of a walk near a country house, and of *a close walk in the wood*, have been used for Barnwell's murder of his uncle. Thorowgood, his daughter and Blunt enter through a door in front of the proscenium arch. Blunt reports the result of the trial. Thorowgood shows that he can pity Barnwell. They go out.

There is in effect no action in this scene. Against an appropriate background, the appropriate sentiments are reported and described. Then the backcloth is drawn (the main curtain, of the proscenium arch, could alternatively be used), and at a further depth in the stage, though still not at its end, is the painted scene of a dungeon, and Barnwell discovered in it. (The dungeon painting, like the prison wall, is from stock; it was commonly used. There are now many professional scene-painters.)

We see Barnwell reading, in the dungeon. Thorowgood re-enters, in front of the proscenium arch, by a door. He is then in a position to indicate Barnwell, from the audience's point of view:

THOROWGOOD: There see the bitter fruits of passion's detested reign and sensual appetite indulged – severe reflections, penitence and tears.

It is a tableau; indeed very much like a moral painting. Then Thorowgood moves through the proscenium arch and is in the dungeon:

BARNWELL: My honoured, injured master, whose goodness has covered me a thousand times with shame, forgive this last unwilling disrespect! indeed I saw you not.

THOROWGOOD: 'Tis well; I hope you were better employed in viewing of yourself.

Here, two elements of the performance situation – the 'viewing', and Thorowgood's conventional step through an empty space into the dungeon, so that Barnwell has no unlocking of doors to bring him to what is expected to be a proper attention – are used for the moral demonstration. A table and lamp are set by the scene. Thorowgood and Barnwell speak of repentance, and then Thorowgood leaves. The Keeper and Trueman enter, in front of the arch. The same process is repeated, but now in reverse:

KEEPER: Sir, there's the prisoner.
BARNWELL: Trueman – my friend, whom I so wished to see! yet now he's here I dare not look upon him. [*Weeps*]

The keeper has gone out again. Trueman watches and then moves through to the dungeon:

TRUEMAN: O Barnwell! Barnwell!
BARNWELL: Mercy, mercy, gracious heaven! For death, but not for this, I was prepared.

They talk and then Trueman, in his turn, leaves, called from the front of the stage by the Keeper. Barnwell, alone in the dungeon, confesses:

I now am – what I've made myself.

The fixed picture is again arranged. And now Trueman re-enters, with Maria, and the indication is made again, from the front of the stage:

TRUEMAN: Madam, reluctant I lead you to this dismal scene. This is the seat of misery and guilt. Here awful justice reserves her public victims. This is the entrance to shameful death.

And they move in again, to speak to Barnwell.

The bell tolls, and the Keeper and Officers come through from the front of the stage to the dungeon. Barnwell makes his last speech, moving forward out of the presumed space of the dungeon to the front of the stage, attended by the Keeper and Officers, and by Trueman and Maria. It is the conventional last speech of the condemned penitent. At its end, Barnwell is led by the Keeper and Officers to go out through a door on one side of the stage, while Trueman and Maria, looking back, go out of the other.

And now the dungeon scene is drawn back, and beyond it, *at the farther end of the stage*, is the place of execution, with the gallows set up and a crowd gathered. Lucy and Blunt enter, in front of the proscenium arch, at one side, and then Barnwell and Millwood, guarded and with their executioner, enter, after a warning cry, from the other. Again, with the painted scene prepared, the indication is made:

BARNWELL: See, Millwood, see, our journey's at an end.

They remain at the front of the stage, with the gallows beyond them, and speak of the possibility of mercy. Then, as they are led through the depth of the stage to their execution, Trueman enters, and he and Lucy take over the physical and moral indication of what is happening beyond them. Then the proscenium curtain is drawn, at the moment before execution, and Trueman turns with his moral to the audience:

... Unless we mark what drew their ruin on
And, by avoiding that – prevent our own.

## *Caste* by T. W. Robertson; 1867

In their different ways, both *The Plain Dealer* and *The London Merchant* show the persistence of older dramatic and theatrical conventions – flexibility of place, with the stage as an open playing area; flexibility of speech convention, allowing elements of direct address and commentary – within a process of adaptation to particular and local forms based on other structures of feeling: the idiom of Restoration talk, with its radical scepticism built into the form of the play; the sentimental morality of early bourgeois drama, combining the exposition of intransigence with the sketch of individualized suffering. This mixture of elements is again evident in the transitional structures of the theatres: the proscenium arch, but also the open stage, though shrinking in size, in front of it; the elaborately painted scenes, but these still temporary and mobile, allowing constant movement from place to place. The most important structural contrast between *The Plain Dealer* and *The London Merchant* is the dramatic use of openness and mobility in the Wycherley play, and the change towards a series of isolated and indicated pictures or tableaux in Lillo. By the time of Robertson's *Caste*, this structural change has been taken very much further, and the theatre itself has been adapted to correspond to this fixed and serial structural emphasis.

### THE CONDITIONS OF PERFORMANCE

*Caste* was first produced at the Prince of Wales Theatre on Saturday, 6 April 1867. It was a period of very rapid expansion in the theatre, bringing many earlier developments to a new climax. Many new theatres were being built in London; the Prince of Wales itself had only recently been reconstructed. Audiences were much larger, and were now more definitely middle-class. The time of performance had moved from the afternoon, in the Restoration, through the late afternoon and early evening in the eighteenth century, to the evening and late evening. Plays were put on for runs of some weeks, and then often went on tour, to a chain of provincial theatres.

Inside the theatre, stalls have replaced the pit benches, and an orchestra is placed between them and the stage. The steady pressure on the stage in front of the proscenium arch has pushed it now right back, inside what is consciously arranged as a picture-frame. The auditorium is now very much larger overall, and rises in several tiers of boxes and galleries. On the stage, the scenery has developed into a 'set': a fixed place, elaborately built and furnished. Gas lighting, since 1820, has allowed more elaborate and selective control of its illumination. The actors, in their set and behind their picture-frame, are also behind more elaborate footlights, in a tableau illuminated and watched from a consciously separated and dimmed auditorium. A new figure takes control of this stage: the stage-manager, whom Robertson is said to have invented: the forerunner of the producer or director.

### THE TEXT

*Caste* is written in three acts: the set of the third repeating the first. The working and published text is full of detailed directions on sets, properties, costumes and effects. It opens with detailed diagrams of the 'interiors', with a system of numbering of doors and 'grooves' (the marks of the scenic flats). With this notation, Robertson directs the disposition of his actors, at precise points on the stage, in virtually every move in the action, and in particular in the achievement of opening and closing 'pictures':

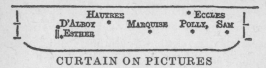

CURTAIN ON PICTURES

Every physical and visual detail of the performance has been, as far as possible, exactly described.

D'Alroy, an aristocratic officer, courts the actress daughter of Eccles, an unemployed and drunken workman. He marries her, and outrages his mother, the Marquise. He is reported killed on service in India. Eccles spends the money left for Esther, and she, now with D'Alroy's child, becomes poor, moves back to her father's house, and eventually back to the theatre. Her sister, Polly, who has flirted with D'Alroy's friend Hautree, marries a plumber, Sam Gerridge. D'Alroy returns, unexpectedly alive, and this and the child reconcile the Marquise to the marriage. These are the problems of 'caste', and of the relations between official and natural 'breeding'.

The play is written in a detailed imitation of conversation, especially in the matter of contrast of accents. At certain demonstrative points it breaks into exclamations about caste, in something of the manner of Lillo, but in general is written to fit in with the prescribed set and costumes and representative activities in a total imitation of characteristic behaviour.

PERFORMANCE

We can look at the ending of the first act. The performance can be set down exactly as Robertson has written it:

94

## DESCRIPTION OF THE PLATES

*Plate 1.* The ancient theatre and temple of Apollo, in the sacred precinct of Delphi, overlooking the valley of the Plistus. The differences of design, from the original Theatre of Dionysus at Athens, show in the shape of the orchestra and the more elaborate stage buildings. Changes of this kind were a feature of the development of the theatre after the fifth century B.C.

*Plate 2.* A possible picture of a medieval circular theatre, from a manuscript *c.* 1400, in the Bibliothèque de l'Arsenal, Paris, known as the Térence des Ducs. Mr Southern, in *Medieval Theatre in the Round*, argues that the upper half shows a circular theatre (it is marked *Theatrum*) with a scaffold, actors, and audience.

*Plate 3.* Detail, showing God and Angels flanked by musicians, on a scaffold approached by a ladder, with a second scaffold to the right, from Jean Fouquet's miniature of the martyrdom of St Apollonia, in the Musée Condé, Chantilly; *c.* 1455.

*Plate 4.* The theatre at Orange, Vaucluse, one of the best preserved examples of a Roman theatre, with auditorium and a scenic wall 103 metres long and 35 metres high. The detail of the scenic wall has been imagined by the architect Caristie.

*Plate 5.* To be compared with Plate 4: the permanent architectural frontispiece of the Farnese theatre at Parma, Italy, designed by Aleotti in 1618, and a characteristic Renaissance court theatre. While it recalls aspects of the Roman scenic wall, the shape of a stage beyond a proscenium arch is also prefigured.

*Plate 6.* A view of the auditorium of the second Drury Lane Theatre, London, in 1794. The audience is greatly increased, and the pit is pushing the stage back towards the proscenium arch, though one vertical line of boxes still abuts on the stage. Print by Richard Philips.

*Plate 7.* The new Gaiety Theatre, London, in 1869, showing the now marked separation between audience and stage, and the retreat of the stage behind the proscenium arch and its curtains. From the *Illustrated London News* of 1869.

*Plates 8–11.* Stills from the sequence of Bergman's *Wild Strawberries* discussed in the text (see pp. 166–70).
Plate 8: Isak Borg, in the car with his daughter-in-law Marianne, at the moment where he goes to sleep and begins to dream.
Plate 9: Borg in front of his examiner, Alman, with the text written on the blackboard, and the microscope on the desk.
Plate 10: Borg's wife, holding the mirror, near the end of the scene in the clearing, as she speaks of telling her husband and of his response.
Plate 11: Borg, at the cradle, with the dark jagged branches above him.

*Plate 12*. A setting by Terence Gray for *Antigone* at the Festival Theatre, Cambridge. As director of the theatre from 1926 to 1933, Gray opposed 'the old game of illusion and glamour'. There was no proscenium in the theatre, and there were already available levels of stage, forestage, and steps to the auditorium. Gray's setting adds to the levels in a modern set which is directed, not to representation, but to the creation of a playing area.

*Plate 13*. A setting for a production of Hauptmann's *The Weavers*, with music by Nejedly, at the J. K. Tyl Theatre, Plzen, Czechoslovakia, in 1961. This shows not only the use of a stage set to create a playing-area rather than a representation, but a use of lighting both to define further areas of the stage and to create a dramatic image of the play: at once the weavers' shuttles and a prison.

I

2

3

4

5

6

7

10

11

12

13

[*Knocks R.U.E. off.*]

SAM: There! you must open the door – it's the postman.

SALLY: [*to window*] No, I needn't! [*Lifts window.*] Here, postman, this way! [*Receives letter at window.*] Oh, thank you! [*Comes down centre*] It's for you, Esther! [ESTHER *rises*]

ESTHER: For me? [*Takes letter, left centre front*] From Manchester. [*Opens it*]

D'ALROY: Manchester?

ESTHER: Yes, I've got the engagement. Four pounds!

D'ALROY [*suddenly*]: Esther, you shan't go! Stay with me, and be my wife!

ESTHER: Your wife! [*About to fall in his arms, but shrinks away*] What will the world – your world say?

D'ALROY: Damn the world! [*Embraces her*] You are my world! Stay with your husband, Mrs D'Alroy!

SAM [*to* POLLY]: Miss Eccles, let me out!

POLLY [*back to R.2 E door, tantalizes Sam with key*]: Shan't shan't – shan't – shan't – shan't!

[SAM *to window, centre in (flat) back wall, leaps out.*]

POLLY: Oh Sam, Sam! dear Sam! You'll break your neck! [*To window*]

SAM [*looks through railings, visible beyond window, laughs*]: Aah!

[*Latch of door R.2 E shaken. Then knock on it.*]

[ESTHER *starts from* D'ALROY'S *arms, shudders, goes up to get key of* POLLY, *crosses to R.2 E, pauses, unlocks door, then across to table, left.*]
[*Enter* ECCLES *R.2 E, drunk, hat on back of head, etc., staggers down right to chest of drawers, at 1 E looks around 'mooning'.*]

*Curtain on:*

| *Eccles* | *Polly* | *Sam* | *Esther.* *D'Alroy* |
|----------|---------|-------|---------------------|
| (R) | (Window) | (3 E without) | (Left Centre) |

*If the curtain is called up again,* ESTHER *is by* D'ALROY, POLLY *pulls window down to prevent* SAM *looking in.*]

### COMMENT

As a play, though widely successful and influential, *Caste* is a curious combination of wholly finished theatrical writing and essentially unfinished dramatic writing. Indeed the minutely prescribed behaviour, backed up by precise rehearsal and repetition, creates a kind of action which supports the limitation of the speech to information and exclamation, and makes it part of the whole dimension of characteristic behaviour. This is the full arrival of theatrical naturalism, but not yet of dramatic naturalism, which had to wait for new major writers. What has then also to be said, however, is that Robertson totally accepts and writes his form. This was not, as we shall see, by any means always the case later, in plays otherwise much more substantial. The interest of *Caste* is that Robertson prescribes in his writing, at the very time of his own invention of stage-management, the detailed directions for performance which would later pass to the new and separate figure of the producer or director.

### *Hamlet* and *The Feast at Solhoug*

Before we follow through this development, by looking at Stanislavsky's production of Chekhov's *The Seagull*, it will be useful to see what had happened to another kind of dramatic and theatrical action, which in a way links the Elizabethan with the naturalist theatre, and which is of special interest because, in its late and decadent form, it is part of the early work of the dramatic genius who later created the serious naturalist drama: Henrik Ibsen. The scenes are the duel in *Hamlet* (in modern editions, part of Act V, Scene ii: lines 212–348) and the goblet scene in Ibsen's *The Feast at Solhoug* (1855; Act III).

## THE DUEL SCENE IN 'HAMLET'

The scene in *Hamlet* opens with the kind of action of which we have already seen several examples. Claudius joins the hands of Hamlet and Laertes, and each in turn speaks, formally. Their speeches contain the whole of the action at this point. By *action*, here, we must understand the pattern of the whole play, as this scene emphasizes it: not only stating the present situation, but gathering up what is relevant that has preceded it, and casting a shadow forward to what will follow. The assembly of what has already passed appears in Hamlet's lines:

> If Hamlet from himself be ta'en away,
> And, when he's not himself, does wrong Laertes,
> Then Hamlet does it not; Hamlet denies it.
> Who does it then? His madness; if't be so,
> Hamlet is of the faction that is wrong'd;
> His madness is poor Hamlet's enemy.

This is not a speech of self-justification (as Dr Johnson read it, and wished Hamlet had made a better excuse), but is in the main a speech 'beyond character': a patterned statement of a major element in the play as a whole. The return to directness comes in the next words, which also cast a shadow towards the events that will soon follow: again not mainly with relation to Hamlet alone, but rather to the whole situation:

Sir, in this audience,
Let my disclaiming from a purposed evil
Free me so far in your most generous thoughts
That I have shot mine arrow o'er the house
And hurt my brother.

This element is completed in part of Laertes' answer:

. . . I do receive your offer'd love like love,
And will not wrong it;

and in Hamlet's reply:

I embrace it freely,
And will this brother's wager frankly play.

In the pattern of these speeches, the essential action, and its
issue, are already contained: both stated, and tragically fore-
shadowed. Within this, the element of the immediate situation is contained in the earlier part of Laertes' reply:

in my terms of honour
I stand aloof, and will no reconcilement.

The whole structure of these introductory speeches contains,
in fact, all the necessary elements of the action.

But now the scene turns to the separate performance of this
action; to *action*, in fact, in a different sense. The speech
becomes, not that which contains the action, but that which is
written to accompany the action: to punctuate it, to forward
it, and to explain. The physical action is dominant, and essentially separate; the speech is not its embodiment, but its
commentary:

H.: Give us the foils. – Come on.
L.:                                             Come, one for me.

. . .

L.: This is too heavy; let me see another.
H.: This likes me well. – These foils have all a length?

As the stage direction indicates (and the dramatic speech does no more): *they prepare to play.*

At the beginning of the scene, the properties have been set:

> [*A table prepard, Trumpets, Drums and officers with Cushions, King, Queene, and all the state, Foiles, daggers, and Laertes, with other attendants.*]

Claudius announces the conduct of the duel, in what is essentially an explanation of the physical action and effects. As he drinks to Hamlet, there are *trumpets the while*, and the duel begins:

> Come on, sir.
>> Come, my lord.
>>> One.
>>>> No.
>>>>> Judgement.
>
> A hit, a very palpable hit.

The fencing, of course, is expertly done; the Elizabethan actor was trained to it; and it is in itself, here, a sufficient display. As the hit is announced, effects underline it (in the alternative directions: *Drum, trumpets, and shot. Florish, a peece goes off*). And now Claudius puts poison in the cup:

> Hamlet, this pearl is thine.

But the cup is not to be drunk yet:

H.: I'll play this bout first; set it by awhile.
Come: another hit; what say you?
L.: A touch, a touch, I do confess.

All the dramatic speech remains commentary, as the Queen offers her napkin to Hamlet, and then takes the poisoned cup.

K.: It is the poisoned cup! it is too late.

99

For she has drunk, and is now wiping Hamlet's face. Then:

H.: Come, for the third, Laertes . . .
L.:                                   . . . Come on.

Again, as the stage direction puts it: *Play*.

O.: Nothing, neither way.
L.: Have at you now!

    [*In scuffling they change Rapiers.*]

K.: Part them! they are incensed.
H.: Nay, come again.
O.:                     Look to the queen there, ho!

The queen has fallen, poisoned by the cup; and now again
the action veers. Both Laertes and Hamlet are bleeding, and
Laertes recalls the kind of speech of the earlier part of the
scene:

L.: Why, as a woodcock to mine own springe, Osric;
        I am justly kill'd with mine own treachery.

But the physical situation is already so complicated that the
main part of the dramatic speech must still be commentary:

Q.:                     O my dear Hamlet –
    The drink, the drink! – I am poison'd.

Laertes explains the poisoned rapier, and its exchange, and
then:

L.: I can no more, – the king – the king's to blame.
H.: The point envenom'd too!
    Then, venom, to thy work!

He *hurts the King*, and then forces the poisoned cup on him.
The King dies, and Laertes comments:

L.:                   He is justly served.
   It is a poison temper'd by himself –

The physical action, with the speech as commentary, is now complete, and in its place the full dramatic action returns, with Hamlet's words (recalling the earlier *Sir, in this audience*):

> You that look pale and tremble at this chance,
> That are but mutes or audience to this act,
> Had I but time – as this fell sergeant, death,
> Is strict in his arrest – oh, I could tell you –
> But let it be . . .

The speech and action which embody the death of Hamlet are again single and united. The rhythm of the verse catches with the dying breath, but it is the single movement of the dramatic speech that is now again the action:

> . . . If thou didst ever hold me in thy heart,
> Absent thee from felicity awhile,
> And in this harsh world draw thy breath in pain,
> To tell my story –

> . . . But I do prophesy the election lights
> On Fortinbras; he has my dying voice;
> So tell him, with the occurrents, more and less,
> Which have solicited – the rest is silence.

HOR.: Now cracks a noble heart – Good night, sweet prince,
   And flights of angels sing thee to thy rest.

Here once again, although the speech contains the action, we have that deliberate concentration of feeling, the emphasis of a rhythmical pattern, which has already been several times noted in earlier drama. And what is now important is to distinguish it from the kind of speech that preceded it, in this scene. It is often said, by modern critics, that the difference between modern drama and the older forms is that in the former the stage directions are separately printed, while in the latter they are often spoken aloud. But this sort of distinction springs from a very specialized idea of *action*; in this scene from *Hamlet* we have been able to see two kinds of 'spoken action'; one a commentary on a separate action, that serves, at times, as 'spoken stage directions'; the other a form of *acted speech*, containing the action certainly, and in that sense a kind of 'stage direction', but because the speech and action are one, essentially different from what 'stage direction' now implies. The action is not spoken aloud, in the older plays, as a kind of clumsy device, but because the speech is the action, and the action the speech. It is only where the action becomes separate, a thing in itself, that one can talk of 'spoken stage directions', and these are then more accurately described as commentary. This famous scene in *Hamlet* shows very well an element of performance of which much more will be heard: the spectacular action, which breaks out and is isolated from the verbal pattern; and when this begins to happen, both the idea of 'stage directions', and the whole idea of dramatic speech, undergo a far-reaching change. In *Hamlet* it is still an interlude, to a considerable extent controlled by the different kind of dramatic action that surrounds it; but in the years to come this kind of interlude was to become, at times, the dominating element of the whole drama.

### THE GOBLET SCENE IN 'THE FEAST AT SOLHOUG'

We need look only briefly at the scene from Ibsen's *The Feast at Solhoug* – a very early play which is, of course, in no way representative of the best of his work. On the small stage of the theatre at Bergen where it was first performed, the

scene represents the hall at Solhoug. There is a backcloth of
a fiord landscape, and in front of it, forming a passageway
and with a central entrance, a painted wall. There are painted
shutters along the wings, and tables on either side. The table
at right front stands under a leaded bay-window. The scene
is played in semi-darkness, lighted by a few oil-lamps; it
is just before dawn, and at the end of the act the sun will rise
and shed its light into the hall. Medieval costume is worn by
the actors.

The persons in this scene are Margit, the wife of Bengt
Gauteson, the Master of Solhoug; her sister, Signe; Gudmund
Alfson, their kinsman; and a House-Carl. But the principal
actor, one might almost say, is Margit's inherited goblet.

Gudmund and Margit are young, and when Gudmund
went away, some years before, they drank together from the
goblet to his happy return. But in the interval Margit has
married the old 'hill-king', Bengt Gauteson, 'for his gold'.
Now Gudmund has returned, and has shown Margit a phial
of poison, which was intended for poisoning the King of
Norway, in a plan by a young knight and the princess who
loved him but who was betrothed to the King. In the Second
Act, Gudmund takes out the phial again, to throw it away,
but Margit takes it from him and, while pretending to throw it
away herself, hides it. Then, in the third act, the husband,
Bengt, while taunting Margit with Gudmund's love for her,
asks her to fill the goblet with wine. She does so, and, as the
taunting continues, *involuntarily takes out the phial.*

BENGT: Ha, it may be that at first Gudmund will look
   askance at me when I take you in my arms; but that, I
   doubt not, he will soon get over.
MARGIT: This is more than woman can bear. [*She pours the
   contents of the phial into the goblet, goes to the window, and
   throws out the phial.*]

She hesitates, but at last tells him that his drink is ready and goes out. The goblet stands on the table under the window. Bengt goes across to it, and lifts it to drink.

But now, suddenly, the House-Carl hurries in: to tell Bengt that an armed band of his enemies is approaching the house. Bengt puts the goblet down again on the table, and rushes out at the back, with the House-Carl, to arm himself. The hall is empty for a moment and then, through the door near the table, enter Gudmund and Signe. They are now in love, but Gudmund is outlawed, and must leave the country; and Signe is in danger of being captured by the leader of the armed band approaching the house, who wants her for his wife. They agree to leave together, but first Signe wishes to drink a farewell health to her sister Margit. She takes up the goblet from the table. Gudmund agrees to drink it with her.

They are about to do so, when Gudmund suddenly recognizes the goblet as the one in which he and Margit had drunk at their former parting. No one else must drink from it, he says, and he reaches across the table to the window and empties out the goblet's contents. Then he and Signe prepare to hurry away, but before they can leave, Margit comes in, opposite them. Gudmund is still holding the goblet in his hands:

MARGIT: The goblet! Who has drunk from it?

GUDMUND [*confused*]: Drunk –? I and Signe – we meant –

MARGIT [*screams*]: O God, have mercy! Help! Help! They will die.

GUDMUND [*setting down the goblet*]: Margit –!

SIGNE: What ails you, sister?

MARGIT [*towards the back*]: Help! help! Will no one help?

[*The* HOUSE-CARL *rushes in from the back.*]

CARL [*calls in a terrified voice*]: Lady Margit! Your husband –!

MARGIT: He – has he, too, drunk –!

GUDMUND [*to himself*]: Ah! now I understand –
CARL: Knut Gesling has slain him.
SIGNE: Slain!
GUDMUND [*drawing his sword*]: Not yet, I hope. [*Whispers to* MARGIT] Fear not! No one has drunk from your goblet.
MARGIT: Then thanks be to God, who has saved us all! [*She sinks down on a chair to the left.*]

The scene may read now almost as parody, yet it is instructive. The poisoned goblet has become, in our own time, a recognized cliché of this kind of action, so that it is almost shorthand for melodrama. But if we are to understand this kind of drama, we must ask ourselves how often we have enjoyed a play or film in which the action is essentially similar, but has a more up-to-date fatal object. The bomb in the suitcase, the test-tube of germs, the radioactive particle are, I suppose, the normal equivalents. For the essential method we are considering is a dramatic action which has become wholly separate and self-sufficient. It is a complicated and exciting action; its process is the manufacture, usually through an object, of one after another exciting situation. For the kind of dramatic movement which we saw in the Greek and medieval performances, this different kind of movement has at times been wholly substituted. The necessary moves in the scene from *Hamlet* – the Queen's taking up the cup meant for Hamlet; the exchange of the poisoned rapier – are of the same kind as those in the scene from *The Feast at Solhoug*. The duel itself, in *Hamlet*, is the flaring into spectacular physical terms of a verbal quarrel; it enacts, at a different level, what has already been totally and substantially enacted, in experience. In the scene from *The Feast at Solhoug*, this major substance has gone. Indeed, the dramatic speech, at certain points, is deliberately contrived to increase the confusion. To Margit's question, *Who has drunk from it?* the answer could as easily have been: *Nobody. I emptied it out of the window.* The House-Carl might as easily have given his full message, *Your husband is slain*, as have been interrupted after *husband* with *He – has he, too, drunk!* I am not arguing the matter in terms of probability, but only in terms of the dramatist's intention. Here, it is clear, Ibsen wants no more of dramatic speech than that it should keep the confusion of the action going. And whenever *action*, in this sense, is given this kind of priority, the whole nature of the performance of drama has, evidently, radically changed.

# 6

## *The Seagull*, by Chekhov; 1898

### THE CONDITIONS OF PERFORMANCE

THE performance here is the first production by Stanislavsky and Nemirovich-Danchenko, at the People's Art Theatre (later known as the Moscow Art Theatre), on 17 December 1898. Chekhov had written *The Seagull* in 1895, and it had been first performed at the Alexandrinsky Theatre in St Petersburg on 29 October 1896, in a production by E. P. Karpov. This production was not successful. Chekhov continued to revise the play until its publication in 1897, and it was meanwhile performed at other theatres in various parts of Russia. The performance at the People's Art Theatre in 1898 is now famous, for it not only established the success of the play, but also made widely known a new method of production. The play remained in the repertory of this first phase of the Moscow Art Theatre until 1905, although the production underwent several changes.

The performance was part of the first season of the People's Art Theatre, and had been preceded by productions of *Czar Fyodor*, *The Sunken Bell*, *The Merchant of Venice*, *The Usurpers*, *Greta's Happiness* and *The Woman at the Inn*. The work of the theatre was conceived as a challenge to the methods of the established theatres; it was, that is to say, a conscious experiment, relying for its direct support on a minority of theatre-goers who were similarly dissatisfied with established methods. This appeal to a conscious minority is of general significance, for it is characteristic of an important part of the modern drama. Already, of course, the theatre-going public, in relation to society as a whole, was itself a section: predominantly the upper and middle classes. The historian of the Moscow Art Theatre (S. D. Balukhaty) writes of the support for the new theatre as coming from the 'more progressive circles of the upper middle classes', and adds:

On the other hand, the nineties of the last century were noteworthy for the awakening of the working classes which brought about a great rise in the intellectual life of the masses of the Russian people and led to a growth of interest in art among those social groups which had hitherto shown no particular interest in it.

This new element was still a distinct minority, however, and the audience for the performance with which we are concerned must be understood as a 'minority audience': that is to say, one drawn from particular groups in society, rather than generally from the community as a whole. On 17 December 1898 there were, as a matter of fact, many empty seats in the auditorium.

The curtained stage and the auditorium are of the type still generally familiar to us; the performance, as is our own normal habit, was in the evening. The experimental approach is one within the normal existing structure of the modern theatre; and the occasion of the performance, when the appeal to a minority audience has been noted, is again that habitual in our own times.

When the curtain is raised, and the lights in the auditorium have been lowered, the stage is seen to be about forty feet wide, and the painted scenery on it rises to about twenty feet. The stage has an apparent depth, at its farthest visible point, about equal to its height, but over much of the stage one does not see back more than about eight feet. The scenery for the first two acts is a painted representation of a park on a country estate; there are at least fifteen tree-trunks, some very close together, immediately visible, and the branches and leaves of these interlock across the top of the scenery, and at the boles there are smaller bushes and undergrowth. Towards the left of the stage, as the audience faces it, an avenue leads back to what appears to be an open summer-house, with a table and chairs in it; this is built with tall columns, of which five are visible. At a number of places under the trees are wooden benches, and one long bench runs directly across the centre of the stage, at its front. Facing this, a little to the right of centre, a curtain some ten feet high, and eight or nine feet across, is hung between two trees. Behind this, as will be later shown, is a temporary stage, which forms part of the action of the play, and beyond it a view of a lake, which the curtain now conceals. In the second act, this small curtain will be down, and in front of where it hung will be a table, with tea things on it, and a few house chairs.

For the third and fourth acts, there is new scenery. The third act represents a dining-room, with a laid table in its centre, and windows that open into the garden beyond; trees in the garden appear in this space. A lamp hangs over the table, from the visible ceiling. There are windows to right and left, with other rooms visible through them. A carpet is on the floor, and a number of other tables, cabinets and chairs are set around, for the most part back against the three walls. On and in these are many smaller objects: lamps, books, ornaments, candlesticks; and a fishing net is standing against the wall. The fourth act represents a drawing-room, with an open doorway, centre, through which another room is visible. Wallpaper and pictures are on the walls, the windows are curtained, and there are several chairs, tables, cabinets, bookstands, a desk. Four lamps are visible, and there is a clock near the fireplace, and books, papers and writing materials on the desk. Of this last room, the designer wrote:

The room had to bear the stamp of impermanency. Outside it is cold, damp, windy; but there is no warmth in the room either . . . I began with the furniture, arranging it in every possible way so as to obtain the effect of mental dis-equilibrium, so that one could see immediately how indifferent the person who lives in that room is to the way the furniture is arranged. If some piece of furniture is in his way, he moves it aside, and does not bother to replace it until someone else finds it is in *his* way. I got the sort of room that made you wish 'to wrap a shawl round you', as one of the actresses put it.

This comment, apart from its particular descriptive relevance, is an indication of a general method: in its multiplicity of detail, each setting is designed to promote the general 'atmosphere' of the play being performed.

In addition to the visible scenery, the producer uses a large number of effects of sound and light. For example, at the beginning of the play:

Darkness, an August evening. The dim light of a lantern on top of a lamp-post, distant sounds of a drunkard's song, distant howling of a dog, the croaking of frogs, the crake of a landrail, the slow tolling of a distant church-bell ... Flashes of lightning, faint rumbling of thunder in the distance.

In a similar way to the scenery, these effects, the producer notes, 'help the audience to get the feel of the sad, monotonous life of the characters'. They are repeated, and varied, at many points in the performance.

The actors, men and women, are dressed in the everyday clothes appropriate to the characters they represent. Their method of dramatic speech is an imitation of the pace and sound of ordinary conversation (with the single exception of a dramatic soliloquy which is performed as part of the play's action). Corresponding to this method of speech, the movement and grouping of the actors are an imitation of the normal everyday actions appropriate to the characters and way of life being represented. The detailed effect of this kind of speaking and movement, in its setting of realistic scenery and realistic

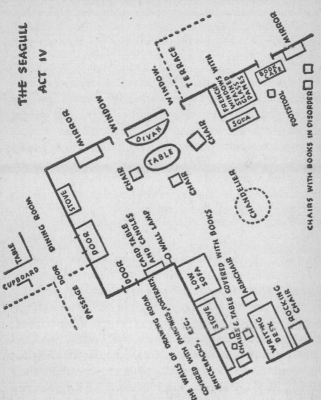

Fig. 5. Stanislavsky's design for Act IV of *The Seagull*

effects of light and sound, is best seen in the study of particular passages from the play, and, as a preliminary to this, we must first look at the general structure of the dramatic text.

## THE TEXT

The text of *The Seagull* contains about 20,000 words. It is arranged in four acts, which, in terms of length, are in the approximate proportion of 9:7:8:10. (cf. Ibsen's *The Wild Duck*, approximately 21,000 words, four acts, in the approximate proportion 5:6:7:11; Ibsen's *Hedda Gabler*, approximately 19,000 words, four acts, in the approximate proportion 10:9:6:5; Chekhov's *The Cherry Orchard*, approximately 21,000 words, four acts, in the approximate proportion 7:5:5:4; Eliot's *The Cocktail Party*, approximately 32,000 words, three acts, of which the first is divided into three scenes, in the proportion 24 (11:4:9):12:10.) As is the general practice with modern texts, the written dramatic speech is accompanied by introductory and parenthetical comment, on the scene, movements and the tone of particular parts of the speech. There are thirteen speaking characters.

The movement of the play's action follows no formal pattern, and is consequently difficult to set out in abstract. Moreover, as is again normal in modern drama, it contains many apparently minor and incidental encounters, which have to be omitted in a summary of the main action, but which are often of equal importance with it in the whole communication of the play. Subject to these limitations, however, the structure of the action may be thus set out:

*Act I*

On a summer evening, a play by Konstantin Treplyov is to be played by Nina Zaryechnaya in the park of the country estate of Peter Sorin, brother of a professional actress, Mme

Arkadina, who is Konstantin's mother. A workman, Yakov, is preparing the stage. The guests include Shamrayev (Sorin's estate agent), his wife Pauline, his daughter Masha; Medvyedenko, a schoolmaster; Dorn, a doctor; Trigorin, a novelist and friend of Mme Arkadina. The performance begins, but is broken off by Konstantin, in anger at a comment by his mother. Nina leaves for her home, and Konstantin goes to try to find her. Masha, who at the beginning of the act has refused a proposal of marriage from Medvyedenko, confesses to Dorn that she loves Konstantin.

## Act II

Mme Arkadina, Dorn, Masha are in the park at midday. Nina comes to them, with Sorin, and later Medvyedenko, Shamrayev and Pauline. Nina is at last left alone, and Konstantin comes to her and lays at her feet a seagull which he has shot. Trigorin comes out, and Konstantin leaves him alone with Nina. Trigorin talks of his writing, and tells her of an idea for a story: a girl 'free and happy as a seagull. Then a man comes along, sees her, and – just for the fun of it – destroys her, like the seagull here'. Mme Arkadina calls Trigorin into the house.

## Act III

In the dining-room of the house. Konstantin has tried to kill himself. Masha tells Trigorin that she has finally agreed to marry Medvyedenko. Nina gives Trigorin, who is going away, a parting present of a medallion. Konstantin comes to his mother, and reproaches her for loving Trigorin; he himself is still desperate because he has failed with Nina. Trigorin comes to Mme Arkadina and asks her to release him for Nina. Arkadina refuses, and they agree to leave together. On their way out, Trigorin returns for a moment, and Nina tells him that she has decided to leave home and become an actress. They arrange to meet in Moscow, and Trigorin kisses her.

## Act IV

In the drawing-room of the house. Two years have passed. Masha is staying in the house, and refuses, for the time being, to go back with her husband to their baby. Sorin, who is ill, is wheeled into the room, where Konstantin normally writes. Konstantin comes in, and after a while talks to Dorn of Nina, who has lived with Trigorin, borne him a child, and been deserted by him. Konstantin has had letters from her, signed 'The Seagull'. Now Arkadina brings in Trigorin, whom she has met at the station. After conversation, all but Konstantin go in to dinner. He is left alone, trying to write. Nina comes in from the garden, and they talk. Konstantin asks her to stay with him, but she refuses – she still loves Trigorin – and goes. Konstantin, again alone, tears up all his manuscripts, and goes into the next room. The others return, and drink and sit down at the card table. Shamrayev brings in the seagull which Konstantin gave to Nina; it has been stuffed, and Shamrayev gives it to Trigorin, who had ordered it. Trigorin does not remember. A noise is heard from the next room, and Dorn goes to investigate. He returns and tells Trigorin to get Mme Arkadina away – Konstantin has shot himself, and is dead.

This is no more than a bare summary of the main action. In most good naturalist plays, and particularly in the case of Chekhov, such a summary of the action produces a very different effect from the whole play. It is in terms of the actual, complicated detail that even the action is to be understood.

## Konstantin and Sorin

My first example from *The Seagull* in performance is from the first act: a dialogue between Konstantin and Sorin, in which Konstantin so predominates that the scene is virtually monologue. It is of considerable importance, from a comparative point of view, to see how this kind of speech is acted.

Konstantin and Sorin are discussing Mme Arkadina, and Konstantin's play. They are on the central bench, immediately behind the footlights, with the whole scene of the park behind them. Sorin is sitting with his back to the audience; he has taken out a small comb, and is combing his beard. Konstantin has lit a cigarette, and is now lying on the bench, facing the audience, with his head on his hand.

SORIN: You have got it into your head that she doesn't like your play, and you are nervous and all the rest of it. Set your mind at rest, your mother worships you.

Konstantin bends down as he lies on the plank, picks a flower, and begins plucking off its petals. Sorin finishes combing his beard, and takes off his hat.

KONST.: She loves me, she loves me not, she loves me, she loves me not, she loves me, she loves me not.

He laughs, and throws down what is left of the flower.

You see, my mother doesn't love me. Why should she? She wants to live, to love, to wear pretty frocks; and I, I am twenty-five years old, and a perpetual reminder that she is no longer young. When I'm not there, she is only thirty-two; when I am, she's forty-three, and she hates me for that.

Sorin is now combing his hair. Konstantin puffs at his cigarette, and shakes off the ash.

She also knows that I don't believe in the stage. She loves the stage; she thinks that she is advancing the cause of humanity and her sacred art; but I regard the stage of to-day as mere routine and prejudice.

Konstantin sits up on the bench, still facing the audience. He picks several blades of grass, and begins tearing them, nervously. Sorin has finished combing his hair, and now begins to untie his cravat. As Konstantin goes on, his speech becomes more and more agitated, the words following each other rapidly, his gestures with the grass and the cigarette more violent.

When the curtain goes up, and the gifted beings, the high priests of the sacred art, appear by electric light, in a room with three sides to it, representing how people eat, drink, love, walk and wear their jackets; when they strive to squeeze out a moral from the flat, vulgar scenes and the flat, vulgar phrases, a little tiny moral, easy to comprehend and handy for home consumption, when in a thousand variations they offer me always the same thing over and over again – then I take to my heels and run, as Maupassant ran from the Eiffel Tower, which crushed his brain by its overwhelming vulgarity.

Sorin has now retied his cravat, and is straightening it.

SORIN: We can't get along without the stage.

Konstantin, in disgust, slaps his leg nervously, gets up and bends over Sorin, trying to convince him. He beats his breast in his agitation.

KONST.: We must have new formulae. That's what we want. And if there *are* none, then it's better to have nothing at all.

He waves his hand, swings himself over the plank of the bench, and begins to pace nervously up and down the stage. There is a pause of five seconds. After pacing up and down, Konstantin calms down a little, walks up to the place he occupied before, looks at his watch, and sits down astride the bench. Sorin has replaced his hat, and still sits with his back to the audience.

KONST.: I love my mother. I love her dearly ...

The scene continues.

This example is a particularly interesting one, because the performance of the scene, as it has been described, rests not on one text, but on two: first, the text of Chekhov's play; and second, the 'production score' which Stanislavsky prepared for it. The dramatic speech is Chekhov's, but most of the actions which accompany it are Stanislavsky's. In Chekhov's text, there are in fact only three explicit directions of action in the scene we have been examining. These are: Konstantin, plucking the petals off a flower; Konstantin, laughs; Konstantin, looking at his watch. These, as we have seen, are retained by Stanislavsky. But the rest of the action is neither indicated, nor determined, by the text. Its sources vary: Sorin's combing his beard and hair, and retying his cravat, come from a previous conversation:

KONST. [*puts his uncle's cravat straight*]: Your hair and beard are all rumpled. You ought to have them cut, don't you think.

SORIN [*smoothing out his beard*]: It's the tragedy of my life. Even when I was young I always looked as if I had taken to drink and all the rest of it. Women never loved me.

Stanislavsky has seized on this, and has prolonged it throughout the subsequent exchange. This is a very good example of the method of this kind of performance: because while the various actions given to Sorin are in a sense based on (or can be derived from) this earlier exchange, the point is that they continue throughout the subsequent long speeches of Konstantin, and so become part of the action accompanying *his* speech. This then helps to determine the effect of what Konstantin is saying. So a kind of action derived from, or suggested by, one place in the text, is used as accompanying action in the performance of another. Within this convention, each movement, gesture and grouping is explanatory; but here the explanation accompanies the speech of another. The importance of this can be seen when it is set beside the action given to Konstantin. The act of looking at his watch has already been twice mentioned previously: he is anxious, as he says, that the play will not start late. The plucking of the flower-petals is related to its particular speech: 'she loves me, she loves me not'. The laugh is when this count appears to prove that his mother does not love him. But on this basis, a whole scheme of action has been devised: the nervous smoking, the tearing of blades of grass, the pacing up and down, the poses on the bench, the nervous slapping of his leg, the beating of his breast. Of course if he is to pluck the petals of a flower he has to pick it first, but all the other actions derive, not from the text, but from a conception of his character suggested by the whole play. Stanislavsky explains:

I cannot help thinking that all through this scene Konstantin is very excited. The performance of his play is to him an event that is of decisive importance to his future career. It is not for nothing that he is in such a nervous state after its failure. The more jumpy and agitated he is now, the stronger will his mood of despair be after the failure of his play.

This is plausible, of course, although it is by no means the only way of reading the scene. But what is important is its essentially different conception of dramatic action. The principle is 'the kind of thing this character might, in all probability, be doing at this point' rather than 'the kind of action that will properly embody this particular dramatic speech'. Any *direct* relation between speech and action has then been abandoned. Instead, the action is related to 'what is behind the whole play', a reading of character and theme which has to be built up as it were separately from the dramatic speech. The consequences of this change are far-reaching.

Two further points should be noted. The first is a distinction

between two kinds of 'probable accompanying action'.
There is action like the tearing of the blades of grass, which is
probable if you conceive the character to be agitated, and
there is action like Sorin's untying his cravat, which is probable in the sense that he has to listen to a long speech by Konstantin and must presumably be doing something meanwhile.
In neither case does the particular action necessarily follow
from the speech; but there is an evident difference of degree of
relevance. The grass-tearing is relevant, given the assumption
of agitation; but sitting on the bench, smoking, and so on,
are merely 'something for the characters to do while they
talk'. The smoking is particularly interesting, for its first
introduction, by Sorin, from whom Konstantin later lights
his own cigarette, is described by Stanislavsky in these words:

A pause of ten seconds. Sorin rocks on the bench, and hums, *or*
whistles, *or* strikes a match and lights a cigarette.

The italics are mine, but they are hardly needed to enforce
the point that whatever action is finally decided upon is
merely 'something for the character to do'. There is a crucial
distinction between action of this kind, and action which,
even where generalized from the whole play, is mimetic in
the sense that it aims to embody a precise state of feeling.

The second point relates to Konstantin's speech about the
stage. As it reads, in the text, where it is accompanied by no
internal or external directions for action, it may reasonably
be taken in a number of different ways. It may be simply the
'wild talk' of a neurotic young man; or, at the other extreme,
it may be intended to make a definite and serious point about
a particular kind of drama. That Stanislavsky chose the first
alternative may, in view of the argument in the speech, be
significant. But the point is that, as the text stands, the speech
could quite legitimately be delivered, and acted, quite

differently. Instead of tearing up grass and talking violently, the producer could as easily have directed:

Konstantin stands very still. His voice has lost its previous agitation, and he speaks slowly and seriously, with real and evident conviction. Sorin listens attentively.

I am not concerned with whether this is *more* plausible than the other direction; my point is that there is nothing in the text to allow, or disallow, either, even although their effects are at opposite extremes. Konstantin can be nervous when he talks of his mother, and intent when he talks of the theatre; or nervous in both, or merely eager and lively in both. And, of course, the choice is very far from academic; for whatever action is decided upon – and the text *enforces* none – will of course determine the essential effect of the scene, and its contribution to the effect of the whole play. I would argue myself that the speech could be acted with a definite internal movement: the simple, narrow rhythm of the petal-counting; the mounting excitement of the comment on the mother; the gradual steadying, and the making of definite points, in the comment on the theatre; and then the excitement of 'always the same thing over and over again' reaching its climax in 'I take to my heels and run'. But a reading of the speech in terms of this kind of action – the movements directly governed by the words – is always, in the final analysis, tenuous: not so much because it cannot be reasonably argued from the speech but because the speech itself is set in the movement of the whole play, and hence, necessarily, is determined by its context, in which no necessary relation between speech and action is laid down or was devised.

## Pauline and Dorn

I wish to turn now to a brief example, from which the same general point emerges. It shows very well the context of the play as a whole, to which I have just referred. It is an episode between Pauline, the wife of Shamrayev, and the doctor, Dorn. Here is the text (Act II):

PAULINE [*entreating*]: Eugene, my dearest, my darling, let me leave him and come to you. Time is flying over us; we are no longer young; let us have done with concealment and falsehood before our days are ended.

[*A pause.*]

DORN: I am fifty-five. It's too late to change my way of life.

Now the problem of Pauline's actions is easy enough: she has said, immediately previously, 'See, I am all trembling', and the 'entreating' gives a generalized indication of voice and movement. But what should Dorn do? In the text, the pause before he replies is, as I see it, meant to indicate his hesitation, and his embarrassment, before his necessary refusal. This, on a very small scale, is an example of the situation which frequently occurs in this kind of play: when the full emotion cannot be spoken, and the fact that it cannot be spoken is suggested by a moment of silence, which may also, by implication, communicate something of what cannot be said. The point is that here is a moment of crisis, incidental to the main action, but relevant to the theme, in that it is a variation on the situation of an ardent, entreating love which does not succeed. So much can be reasonably said, but it is clear that, from the text, we do not really understand Dorn's feelings about the proposal; and, although the pause indicates that he either cannot, or is not prepared to, reply at once, we cannot say why this may be – whether indifference or regretful resignation; nor can we say if the reason he offers is the real one, or in what tone – whether kindly or indifferently – he gives it. The text continues:

PAULINE: I know why you refuse. It is because there are other women besides myself who are dear to you. You cannot let them all come to you. I understand. Forgive me; you are tired of me.

[NINA *appears near the house picking flowers.*]

DORN: No, no, I'm not tired of you.

PAULINE: I suffer agonies of jealousy. Of course you are a doctor; you cannot avoid women. I understand.

DORN [*to* NINA, *who comes down*]: How are they getting on?

NINA: Madame Arkadina is crying and Monsieur Sorin has got asthma.

DORN [*rising*]: I must go and give them both some valerian drops.

NINA [*giving him her flowers*]: These are for you.

DORN: Merci bien. [*Goes towards the house.*]

PAULINE [*following him*]: What pretty flowers! [*Near the house, in a low voice*] Give me those flowers! Give me those flowers! [*She tears them up and throws them aside.*]

[*Exeunt, into the house.*]

This continuation of the scene reinforces the statement of Pauline's feelings, which are sufficiently expressed both in words and in a certain kind of action (the violent gesture of destroying the flowers). But again, what of Dorn? The few sentences that he is given to speak are wholly non-committal; his one action, that of going into the house, is similarly neutral, although it might be interpreted as a move to get away from an impossible situation. As the text stands, in fact, we know only what Dorn does; we cannot really know why.

But if we turn to the performance of this scene, the case is very different. When Pauline and Dorn are left together, Dorn

having nothing to do, stands on the plank and walks, balancing himself, from one end to the other. Pauline drinks up her cup of tea at one gulp, and speaks imploringly.

This is the position when she asks him to take her away, and the scene then goes as follows:

> Dorn walks, swaying, on the plank; Pauline, talking excitedly to him, runs after him on the ground. Dorn is very cool and self-composed, and is occupied with his exercises, while Pauline is very excited.

One can see that this piece of action would be very effective. Dorn, having nothing to do, at least does something that we can watch. But the crucial, and planned, effect of this piece of action is to emphasize Dorn's detachment and lack of interest. He continues absorbed in his own voluntary routine, while Pauline, overcome by her feelings, runs beside and below him. This is a variation, in miniature, of the situation between Nina and Konstantin, and between Trigorin and Nina; and it can easily be defended. But the important point about it is that it is a dramatic effect voluntarily created in performance, and bearing only a possible relation to the dramatic text.

## Konstantin and Nina

The scenes we have examined enforce the same general point, but are alternative illustrations of this kind of performance in a scene played between two people. In each scene, one character monopolizes the direction of the dialogue, while the other is relatively passive. In the scene between Konstantin and Sorin, little action is designed for either, but it is not, as we saw, merely a question of designing action for a virtual soliloquy. In this kind of performance, the acting of the passive partner helps to determine the effect of the *other's* speech; it is, in a sense, part of *his* action. In the scene between Pauline and Dorn, more is done to design the action of the leading character, but again action is invented for the other, which in effect equally determines the expression of the whole scene. The two examples are again alike in that the action remains *personal*, there are no elements of performance (within the fixed painted scene) which the actor himself does not create. But this is not the case in the performance as a whole, and I wish now to turn to a final scene, in which there is a different kind of general effect.

The scene is between Nina and Konstantin, in the fourth act. They have looked back over their lives, and Konstantin has again told her that he loves her and depends on her, and has asked her to stay with him. They are in the drawing-room, and Nina runs across to the french window, and puts on her hat and cloak. Konstantin follows her.

KONST.: Nina, why are you doing that? For God's sake, Nina ...

NINA: My trap is at the garden gate ... Don't come and see me out. I'll manage all right.

The text direction here is 'bursts into tears'. The actual performance (Stanislavsky) is as follows. Nina opens the french window to go out; there is a noise of wind rushing into the room. Then Nina stops, leans against the jamb of the door, and bursts into sobs. Konstantin, who is leaning against the lamp-post just outside the door, stands motionless, gazing at Nina. There is a whistling of wind from the open door.

NINA: Give me some water.

This is spoken between her sobs. Konstantin walks back towards the front of the stage, pours some water into a glass (sound of glass knocking against jug), and gives it her. (The only text direction at this point is 'gives her a glass of water'.)

KONST.: Where are you going to?
NINA: Back to the town.

After this question and answer, the sole stage direction is 'pause'. In performance, however, Nina wipes her tears with a handkerchief, and smothers her sobs. Konstantin stands motionless, glass in hand, leaning against the lamp-post, staring lifelessly at one point. 'This', writes Stanislavsky in his production-score, 'is where he really dies'.

Nina comes back into the room, and talks again of her acting. She does not seem to be addressing anyone in particular, but is as if speaking to herself, her gaze fixed on one point. Konstantin stands motionless, and replies in 'a dead voice, without life, without hope'. There is a pause of ten seconds; then a sudden noise in the dining-room, two or three chairs being pushed back. Nina jumps to her feet and runs to the door. (All this action, and the directions for speaking, come from Stanislavsky's score, not Chekhov's text.)

KONST.: Stay here. I'll get you some supper.

This, Stanislavsky observes, is his last hope.

NINA: No, no. Don't see me out; I can find my way. The trap is quite near ... So she brought him here with her? Well, well, it's all one. When you see Trigorin, don't tell him I've been ... I love him; yes, I love him more than ever ... 'A subject for a short story' ... I love him, love him passionately, desperately.

She opens the french windows to go; the howling of wind and the noise of rain is louder than ever (Stanislavsky).

NINA: How pleasant it was in the old days, Konstantin! You remember? How clear and warm, how joyful and how pure our life was! And our feelings – they were like the sweetest, daintiest flowers ... You remember?'

She recites the speech from Konstantin's play. This is done (Stanislavsky) to the accompaniment of the howling of the wind.

NINA: 'Men and lions, eagles and partridges, antlered deer,

geese, spiders, and the silent fishes dwelling in the water, starfish and tiny creatures invisible to the eye – these and every form of life, every form of life, have ended their melancholy round and become extinct. Thousands of centuries have passed since this earth bore any living being on its bosom. All in vain does this pale moon light her lamp. No longer do the cranes wake and cry in the meadows; the hum of the cockchafers is silent in the linden groves . . .'

Here, Chekhov directs, she embraces Konstantin impulsively, and runs out through the french window. In performance (Stanislavsky) she first leans once again against the jamb of the door, and bursts out crying. A pause of ten seconds, during which can be heard the distant tolling of a church bell. Nina gives Konstantin a quick hug and runs out. One half of the door slams – a pane breaks, so powerfully does the wind slam it; then the other half of the french window shuts; the footsteps on the terrace die away. Noise of the wind, tolling of church bell, knocking of night-watchman, a louder burst of laughter in the dining-room next door. For fifteen seconds Konstantin stands without moving, then he lets fall the glass from his hand.

When Konstantin is alone, the text, with stage-directions, runs:

KONST. [*after a pause*]: I hope nobody will meet her in the garden and tell mother. Mother might be annoyed.

> [*For two minutes he silently tears up all his manuscripts and throws them under the table, then unlocks the door Right, and exit.*]

In performance, this becomes:

Konstantin crosses slowly to the writing-desk. Stops. Goes up 10 where his manuscript lies, picks it up, holds it for a moment in his hand, then tears it up. Sits down, picks something up and tries to read it, but tears it up after reading the first line. Falls into a reverie again, rubs his forehead disconsolately, looks round as though searching for something, gazes for a moment on the heap of manuscripts on his desk, then starts tearing them up with slow deliberation. Gathers up all the scraps of paper and crosses over to the stove with them (noise of opening stove door). Throws the scraps of paper into the stove, leans against it with his hand, looking for some time at the flames devouring his works. Then he turns round, something occurs to him, he rubs his forehead, then crosses over to his desk quickly and opens a drawer. He takes out a bundle of letters and throws it into the fire. Walks away from the stove, ponders for a second, looks round the room once more – and walks out thoughtfully, unhurriedly.

The others return, and Trigorin is given the seagull; a few seconds later a shot is heard, and Konstantin is dead.

The effect of this whole scene, in performance, is powerful, and analysis of its effect is virtually explicit in its exposition. Three main points should be noted. First, the presence in Stanislavsky's production score of such comments as 'this is where he really dies'. These, obviously, are not 'stage directions' in any ordinary sense; they are generalized comments on feeling, which have no direct counterpart in words or action, but which inform the actor about the movement of feeling in the whole scene. Second, it is obvious that *general* performance effects – the wind and the rain, the church bell, the breaking of the pane of glass – play a large part in the total effect, although they do not proceed from the text of the play, but, like the stage designs, from a conception of its *atmosphere*. Third, Konstantin's crisis, when he tears up the manuscripts, is played without speech; both text and score prescribe this, and the score breaks down into detail (and to some extent simplifies and alters) the generally indicated action. The action is critical, and has been wholly separated from dramatic speech.

## COMMENT

*The Seagull* is not Chekhov's best play, but, like the earlier naturalist plays of Ibsen, from *The Doll's House* to *Hedda Gabler*, it is a work of very much higher quality than the 'technical naturalism' of a play like Robertson's *Caste*. Ibsen and Chekhov, and Strindberg in plays like *The Father* and *The Dance of Death*, were working with a seriousness and intensity comparable with the greatest literature of their time, and especially comparable with the novel. Ibsen and Strindberg extended their work into other dramatic conventions (often essentially prefiguring the film), but in this period of high naturalism we have some of the major examples of modern dramatic literature, and the problems of convention and performance are then especially important. *Caste* was an event in the theatre, but in any wider view is a sketch. *The Seagull*, like *Hedda Gabler* or *The Father*, is part of an important creation of modern dramatic form.

But then the first point to note is that *Caste*, in a way because of its status as a sketch, was more completely written for performance than *The Seagull* or other comparable major plays. Every detail of Robertson's lifelike representation is prescribed as part of his whole dramatic conception. What has happened, by the time of Chekhov, is very different. First, the figure of the stage-manager has become the creative producer, who takes what he can now think of as a script rather than a play, and builds a production on it. Without the genius of Stanislavsky, the performance of Chekhov's kind of dramatic writing might well have been impossible. But we have then also to remember that when Chekhov saw this kind of production, he 'became very agitated', and insisted that parts of what they were doing were not 'his play' at all. This situation has become characteristic, but it is important that the argument should not degenerate into mutual complaint between dramatist and producer. The only useful question is about the dramatic form.

For, second, what has also happened, in the period of Ibsen, Chekhov and Strindberg, is that the kind of action being written is, in its experience, unusually complex and precise. It is not the presentation of known situations and responses, but the exploration of intense experience, often, characteristically, of a hidden or unexpressed kind. If the stock situations and responses had been there, the problem of performance would have been very much easier. Certain practised conventions – words, rhythms, looks, gestures – would have been directly available. But these plays push beyond this known and recognizable dimension, and the question, not only of performance but of dramatic action, is then acute. Much of the detailed description of atmosphere, character, look, gesture and manner of speech comes in fact from another literary form, the novel, in which this kind of description can be direct. What is at issue, in a play like *The Seagull*, is whether that kind of attention to detail can be translated into dramatic terms; or, to put the question in a harder way, whether the total conception of experience, to which the details contribute, can be imagined and written in a dramatic form.

We have seen, in the way Stanislavsky produced Chekhov's text, a number of cases in which this crucial detail is added or even imposed. But it remains a fact that if the play was to be put on at all, in the terms in which it was written, this kind of addition was inevitable, since the text, at these points, was radically incomplete. What then should Chekhov have done? There is a sense in which, if he had written the full detail which would in any case be necessary, once the play came to that kind of performance, he would have been writing something very unlike any previous dramatic text, and something much more like a novel. Many published plays of this kind open with descriptions of place and characters which are very like the openings of novels. And indeed, once the dramatic conception has to this extent been separated from formal speech and the presented actions which it can directly prescribe or indicate, some such development is inevitable. It is possible to argue that the separation from formal speech was fatal; that it made major drama impossible. But this is clearly not true. We have had many major plays, from just this method, and their creation relates to certain necessarily different kinds of experience, in our own world. The ways in which we now see persons and their relationships, the connections we make between feeling, situation and place, led necessarily to this new dramatic form. Certainly, when we see the formal drama in decay, as in Ibsen before his major innovations, we would not want to argue that serious experience belonged to those surviving conventions. It so clearly belongs with the new conventions, but then the whole difficulty is what, precisely, these should be.

What needs to be emphasized is that these conventions are more than theatrical methods. In a play like *Caste*, what is finally interesting is that there is no tension between the method and the experience: all the available life of the characters, all the life that is important to the dramatist, can be represented and put on the stage; can indeed be wholly written, because no other forces, no other experiences and possibilities, disturb it. The representation of appearances, of what is external and on the surface, can be directly dramatized, in that patient stage dressing and carpentry. In Chekhov or Ibsen, on the other hand, what is visible and directly expressible is no more than a counterpoint to the unrealized life – the inner and common desires, fears, possibilities – which struggles to find itself in just this solidly staged world. When we speak of naturalism, we must distinguish between this passion for the whole truth, for the liberation of what can not yet be said or done, and the confident and even complacent representation of things as they are, that things are what they seem. This latter convention, of the naturalist habit, has been surprisingly durable; it still supports a majority of our drama, in all forms. But the serious and exploring drama, from Ibsen and Chekhov and Strindberg to Brecht and Beckett, was faced always with a contradiction: that what it seemed to make real, in theatrical terms, was what it wished to show as a limited reality, in dramatic terms. All the difficulties of performing Chekhov come from this contradiction. It is what Stanislavsky later recognized as an 'external imaginative truth ... the truth of objects ... the outward image of the actor', when what was being dramatized through these was a quite different dimension of reality.

What the high naturalist drama achieved, at its most successful, was a consciousness of this tension. This is what both Chekhov and Stanislavsky, in their different ways, were trying to write, in that dimension beyond explicit action and speech. Strindberg, in his expressionist experiments, came to drop the immediate dimension – the dressed and furnished stage which was also the limiting reality of a room and its probable behaviour. He created new forms which directly dramatized the experience of tension: as it were a replay of naturalism, but with the characters and scenes distorted by the tension itself. In much subsequent drama, this method has been widely followed and developed. The advanced machinery and lighting of the theatre has been used, not to create the appearances of rooms, but to show, in physical terms, the shape of the dramatic experience. From Strindberg's *Dreamplay* and *Road to Damascus* to Beckett's *Waiting for Godot* this has been a major achievement of the new drama.

In a different direction, there has been a new impulse to clear the stage, to return to the bare boards, the playing area, in which the action creates itself, through words and movement. Such properties as there are do not establish a fixed place, but are means through which the action is created: an evident example is Ionesco's *The Chairs*. The action most often created has an ironic relation to the history of the theatre, in that what is shown is an illusion, a kind of conscious playing, which is offered as a metaphor for the truth about real life. This tendency has culminated in the 'theatre of the absurd'.

On the other hand, clearing the stage, getting rid of its dressing and furniture, has been used for a different dramatic purpose: not illusion as metaphor, but the exposure of illusion, as a critical examination of reality. This has been, outstand-ingly, the method of Brecht: bringing open argument back on to the stage, not within the terms of the ordinary plot, where different points of view are represented within the limits of the created action, but in such a way as to make the action itself open and self-critical. A scene can be replayed, from different points of view, or the actor can step out of his role and look at what he has been saying and doing, or at its consequences.

These are the substantial dramatic developments which I have examined more fully in *Drama from Ibsen to Brecht*. What needs emphasis here, looking at drama in performance, is that the theatre, in its main tendencies, evolved towards a kind of representation, within its picture-frame stage, which could adequately support the drama of what I have called the naturalist habit, but which was in many ways intrinsically unsuitable for the developments after high naturalism: the new forms which were breaking away from fixed places, fixed appearances, single dimensions and external planes. A great deal has been achieved in experimental drama and theatre, within and against these limitations, but many in-herent difficulties, as we shall see, remain, and these have been more evident in a period in which new means of performance, especially in the film, have become dramatically available.

# 7

# Modern Experimental Drama

WE can look at three examples of plays in performance, in the period of major experiment which followed high naturalism. These are *The Family Reunion*, by T. S. Eliot (1939), *The Life of Galileo*, by Bertolt Brecht (1939–47), and *Waiting for Godot*, by Samuel Beckett (1952).

## THE CONDITIONS OF PERFORMANCE

The material and social circumstances of the theatre were very much the same, in this period of varied experiment, as they had been in the late nineteenth century. There had been technical developments, in lighting and machinery, but these moved in the same direction as the earlier modernization of the theatre for spectacle and for naturalism. Some of the most radical experiments had to be carried out in the material apparatus of an earlier dramatic form.

Audiences, also, were predominantly similar to those of the earlier period. The theatre audience was still mainly middle-class, and performances retained, in most cases, the marks of that kind of social occasion. There had, however, been a further development of the theatre of the conscious minority within this audience: the association of certain kinds of experimental work with particular theatres and companies, and then the affiliation to them of particular audiences. It was in such theatres and companies that virtually all important drama of this century originated, but it is then characteristic that when particular plays and dramatists succeeded, they were ordinarily moved to the majority theatres, for commercial reasons. It was then difficult for the minority theatres to pursue any consistent policy over a long enough period to build new general styles and conventions. For this and other reasons, the twentieth-century theatre has been one of great variation in method: a strength in its opportunities for experiment; a weakness in a certain inevitable eclecticism.

Beckett's play was first produced in a very small theatre in Paris. When it became successful it was moved into the ordinary theatres. Brecht's play was written in exile, and after the first production in Zürich was revised for production in the United States, with Brecht working with a company headed by Charles Laughton. Eliot had written *Murder in the Cathedral* for a production at the Canterbury Festival; after its subsequent success in the theatre, he wrote *The Family Reunion* for normal theatrical production.

## *The Family Reunion* by T. S. Eliot; 1939

### THE TEXT

The text of *The Family Reunion* contains about 24,000 words. It is arranged in two parts, of approximately equal length, each divided into three scenes. The scene is a country house in the North of England. The first part is played in 'the drawing room, after tea; an afternoon in late March'; the second part in 'the library, after dinner'.

### Part One, Scene One

The Monchensey family are coming together, in the family house of Wishwood, for the birthday of Amy, Dowager Lady Monchensey, and the homecoming of her son, Harry, Lord Monchensey, after an absence of eight years. Amy insists that 'nothing is changed at Wishwood', but her sister Agatha argues that 'he will find a new Wishwood . . . I mean that at Wishwood he will find another Harry'. Harry's wife has died, at sea, in the intervening years. When he arrives, he sees 'eyes through a window . . . *you* don't see them, but I see them, and they see me'. He is seeing the Furies, who have waited until his return to Wishwood. He believes that he is responsible for his wife's death: 'that cloudless night in the mid-Atlantic, when I pushed her over'. His servant's account is compatible with this. The majority of the family, in chorus, insist on holding tight to a familiar version of the world, against the possibility of a 'dreadful disclosure'.

### Scene Two

Harry's aunt, Agatha, and his childhood companion, Mary, discuss his marriage and his mother's opposition to it. Harry talks to Mary of his return: to his point of departure, but with himself altered. The Furies are very close, and when he calls to them to come out, the curtains part and they are seen. Mary does not see them, and draws the curtains. When he opens them again, the Furies have vanished.

### Scene Three

The other sons are expected. Harry talks to the doctor of murder, and insists that the past is 'unredeemable'. The majority of the family, in chorus, confess their fears of a curse on the house. Agatha prays that the curse may be lifted.

### Part Two, Scene One

Harry talks about his mother and father, to the doctor. — They were never happy together; they separated and the father died abroad. The mother has kept going only for Harry's return. A policeman calls with news of a minor accident to his brother. Harry begins to see the situation at Wishwood as part of a general disorder, and his own disorder as related to it. The chorus says: 'whether in Argos or England there are certain inflexible laws, unalterable'.

### Scene Two

Harry and Agatha talk of his parents. She tells him how his father had wished to murder his mother, just before Harry was born. Agatha stopped him, and Harry is in that sense her child. In beginning to understand his whole situation, Harry sees the Furies again, but now they are outside him; he will leave Wishwood, following them. Agatha steps into the place the Furies have occupied. Harry explains to his mother that he is going away: that the family house, which had seemed a refuge, is where he encountered the whole pattern of guilt; he will go elsewhere, on an unknown journey, following 'the bright angels', the transformed Eumenides.

### Scene Three

Amy blames Agatha for taking her son, as she once took her husband, away from her. With her idea of the future of Wishwood gone, Amy dies. The curse has come to fulfilment, and redemption is possible, as the family reunion breaks up and they 'depart in several directions'.

This is the barest summary. The interest and the difficulty of *The Family Reunion* is that the action takes place on at least two levels: the physical reunion and its declared relationships, which are directly written; the spiritual encounter, and its undeclared but revealed relationships. The complexity of the play is in the consequent relations between these two planes of action, and this is at once a problem of meaning and a problem of drama in performance. We can look at this more closely, in certain parts of certain scenes.

*The Eumenides*

A critical element in the writing and performance of *The Family Reunion* is the dramatic nature of the apparition – of the Eumenides or Furies. There are three crucial phases: in Part One, Scene One, on Harry's arrival; at the end of Part One, Scene Two, between Harry and Mary; and in Part Two, Scene Two, between Harry and Agatha.

In the first of these cases, the apparition is written in this way:

> [*Enter* HARRY]
>
> AMY: Harry!
>
> [HARRY *stops suddenly at the door and stares at the window.*]

This is clearly within a convention of stage behaviour. The unexpected entrance is followed by the unexpected response. Harry stares at the uncurtained windows: the other members of the family, like the audience, see the empty darkness beyond them. Harry's insistence, in this situation, can be bridged by a misunderstanding, on which the local convention is built:

> HARRY: How can you sit in this blaze of light for all the world to look at?
>
> It you knew how you looked, when I saw you through the window!
>
> Do you like to be stared at by eyes through a window?
>
> AMY: You forget, Harry, that you are at Wishwood,
>
> Not in town, where you have to close the blinds.

Several ambiguities are caught in this way: the simple physical difference between town and country windows; the fact that Harry saw the family assembled, from outside, and that it is then his eyes, or any stranger's eyes, which stare through the window, as well as the other eyes he sees staring.

Behind this ambiguity is a further irony: that this family group is being stared at from another direction – that of the audience – and that the opening and closing of the curtains over the windows, at several points in the action, is made to suggest a whole dramatic process: not only the physical reminiscence of the opening and closing of the curtains on the stage, but the metaphor of a world alternately hidden and revealed beyond the life of the family drawing-room.

At this point, however, it is only metaphor, and what is dramatically communicated is Harry's strangeness:

HARRY: Look there, look there; do you see them?
GERALD: No, I don't see anyone about.
HARRY: No, no, not there. Look there! Can't you see them?
    You don't see them, but I see them,
    And they see me.

It is a metaphor supported by a reminiscence. In the epigraph to his first dramatic experiment, *Sweeney Agonistes*, Eliot quoted from a translation of the *Choephoroi* of Aeschylus:

ORESTES: You don't see them, you don't – but I see them.

This direct recall, of the son of the House of Atreus, cannot, of course, be dramatically communicated, in any general way. It is at most a signal to certain members of the audience: a minority of which Eliot was always conscious. Yet equally the reminiscence is not necessary, for this immediate situation. Harry's strangeness – his insistence that, in an idiom of which Eliot is aware, he is 'seeing things' – comes through as revelation of character, and not yet of action. He goes on to acknowledge the continual presence of 'them'; no name is given; they are 'eyes' staring. He asks, within a dramatic situation of explicit character and relationships, why he is seeing them here, for the first time, at this family reunion. And because of this way of writing his speech, the dramatic

gesture, towards the unseen staring eyes, can be shaded off
into the expected family greetings, the exchange of news and
plans. Harry never joins this exchange, at its own level. He
makes his own kind of statement, as if in response to what they
are saying, but the others respond in their own more familiar
terms. Thus:

AMY:                    Nothing has been changed.
HARRY: Changed? nothing changed? how can you say that
  nothing is changed?
  You all look so withered and young.
GERALD:                We must have a ride tomorrow.
  You'll find you know the country as well as ever.

The obvious fact that this speech is then on two unconnecting
planes, connected only verbally by accident or misunderstanding, is of course Eliot's dramatic design: it is this tension
and failure he is writing. At the same time, in the solidity
of the stage drawing-room, and the heavily conventional
naturalist presence of the family, there is a continual problem
of control: as the planes collide, yet there is no collision within
the available action.

In the next scene, this action is different:

HARRY:                 O Mary!
  Don't look at me like that! Stop! Try to stop it!
  I am going. Oh why, now? Come out!
  Come out! Where are you? Let me see you
  Since I know you are there . . .

This begins in the same ambiguity: the words to Mary pass
into the challenge to the Furies.

HARRY: Come out!

  [*The curtains part, revealing the Eumenides in the window
  embrasure.*]

He speaks to them:

HARRY: . . . I tell you, it is not me you are looking at,
   Not me you are grinning at, not me your confidential looks
   Incriminate, but that other person, if person
   You thought I was: let your necrophily
   Feed upon that carcass. They will not go.
MARY: Harry! There is no one here.

[*She goes to the window and pulls the curtain across.*]

When Harry insists that they are still present, and rushes to
open the curtains again: *the embrasure is empty*.

There are two related problems in this scene: of performance, and of dramatic imagination. As Eliot wrote later:

We tried every possible manner of presenting them. We put them
on the stage, and they looked like uninvited guests who had strayed
in from a fancy dress ball. We concealed them behind gauze, and
they suggested a still out of a Walt Disney film. We made them
dimmer, and they looked like shrubbery just outside the window. I
have seen other expedients tried: I have seen them signalling from
across the garden, or swarming onto the stage like a football team,
and they are never right.

We have to remember this (which was indeed obvious before
Eliot so gracefully admitted it) as we read their final appearance, and their replacement by Agatha:

HARRY:                  not just as before,
   Not quite like, not the same . . .

   [*The Eumenides appear.*]

HARRY: . . . This time, you are real, this time, you are outside
me . . .
   Now I see at last that I am following you . . .

[*The curtains close.* AGATHA *goes to the window, in a somnambular fashion, and opens the curtains, disclosing the empty embrasure. She steps into the place which the Eumenides had occupied.*]

Since this transformation is so crucial – of the Furies into the bright angels; of unrealized personal guilt into a religious consciousness of sin – it is very difficult to salvage the play by what seems Eliot's simple expedient, after the difficulties of performance:

They must, in future, be omitted from the cast, and be understood to be visible only to certain of my characters, and not to the audience.

For it is their objective character that is the means of the transformation, as Eliot has written it, and what we really see, behind the difficulty of presentation, is a problem of dramatic imagination and dramatic writing. For without the figures of the Furies, establishing a non-human dramatic reality, the action is essentially incomplete. The hints and guesses, even the intense local expressions and analyses of experience, cannot, on their own, create a dramatic structure in Eliot's terms. His own explanation was that he

should either have struck closer to Aeschylus or else taken a great deal more liberty with his myth . . . Their failure is merely a symptom of the failure to adjust the ancient with the modern.

But this underestimates the problem. It is not in the adjustment or the interpretation of the myth that the real problem arises; it is in the nature of the dramatic action. In many modern plays, the Furies have in fact been successfully presented (compare the *Electra* of Giraudoux or the *Flies* of Sartre). The difficulty, one might say, in *The Family Reunion*, is not the Furies but the 'window embrasure' and its stage-set drawing-room and library. It is the scenic establishment, in the dramatic conception of the play, of a kind of reality, the fully furnished country house, with which not only the Furies, but the whole inner conception and theme, are incompatible. This cannot be solved by excising the Furies. What is really of interest, as a characteristic dramatic problem, is Eliot's insistence on grafting a play of spiritual revelation on to the most enclosed of all theatrical forms: that of the fixed, entering and exiting, country house group.

## The Chorus

The more closely we examine *The Family Reunion*, the greater this incompatibility becomes. The chorus is another example: two uncles and two aunts, from the group, assemble to speak together, beyond this ordinary range:

We do not like to look out of the same window, and see quite a different landscape.
We do not like to climb a stair, and find that it takes us down.
We do not like to walk out of a door, and find ourselves back in the same room.

What is interesting here, in the play's insistence on the unexpected revelation, is that all the images are physical, and are those of a house: the window, the stair, the door. Yet in the fixed room, to which he has committed himself, these are precisely the surprises which cannot dramatically happen; they can only be spoken about, and then the fact that they do not and cannot happen – just as the Eumenides, finally, cannot appear – is a destructive tension within the chosen form. This is released as conscious embarrassment:

Why do we feel embarrassed, impatient, fretful, ill at ease.
Assembled like amateur actors who have not been assigned their parts?
... Waiting for the rustling in the stalls, the titter in the dress circle, the laughter and catcalls in the gallery?

But this is a desperate attempt to head off what is already inevitable. Again, Eliot later recognized this:

> The device of using four of the minor personages, representing the Family, sometimes as individual character parts, and sometimes collectively as chorus, does not seem to me very satisfactory. For one thing, the immediate transition from individual, characterized part to membership of a chorus is asking too much of the actors: it is a very difficult transition to accomplish.

Certainly, but a transition is from something as well as to something, and I know if I had to choose between what are really the West End bit-parts, the aunts and uncles in their 'individual, characterized' existence, and the voice of the chorus, I would have no hesitation: the latter is possible drama, the former simply theatrical padding. Once again, from the initial choice of a leading convention – the country-house play, with its expected furniture and characters – Eliot established a theatrical mode which made his only serious dramatic action crippled or impossible.

## THE REPRESENTATIVE AND THE REAL

It is not only the difficulties; it is what is learned from them. What Eliot brought to the drama was a new and contemporary precision and intensity of speech:

> If you want to know why I never leave Wishwood
> That is the reason. I keep Wishwood alive
> To keep the family alive, to keep them together,
> To keep me alive, and I live to keep them.
> You none of you understand how old you are
> And death will come to you as a mild surprise,
> A momentary shudder in a vacant room.

These are wholly speakable lines, in dramatic performance. What is difficult is their coexistence with

> All that a civilized person needs
> Is a glass of dry sherry or two before dinner.
> The modern young people don't know what they're
>     drinking,
> Modern young people don't care what they're eating;
> They've lost their sense of taste and smell
> Because of their cocktails and cigarettes.
> That's what it comes to.

It is not only the difference in feeling. It is the part of the mind, the level of dramatic reality, that is really in question. This is then a question of writing. Eliot has described his dramatic verse line: 'of varying length and varying number of syllables, with a caesura and three stresses ... the only rule being that there must be one stress on one side of the caesura and two on the other'. This is relatively easy to discern in the first passage quoted; the stresses follow the meaning, in a single tone. In the second passage, the lines can be scanned in this way (though there are at once more difficulties, as in the second or fifth lines), but what is much more important than this abstract point is that the tone of the speech makes that kind of sustained rhythm impossible in practice, because the actor has to do something else with his voice; he has to create, in tags, a character part. The rhythm itself, if strictly followed, pulls these pompous words towards Eliot's familiar and measured gravity, but what the actor has to do comes from the overall characterization, and it is this lighter rhythm which inevitably predominates. And then what is interesting is that Eliot's subsequent choices of convention were, in the verse as in scene and in dialogue, towards the West End, and away from the drama. He excised not only the Furies, but, increasingly, the element which they pointed towards: the conscious presence and intensity, in scene, dialogue and rhythm, of the only action that mattered to him.

## THE VERSE DRAMA EXPERIMENT

Contemporary English verse drama was always, essentially, a *writer's* reform, and this served only to expose many of the inherited difficulties, in the confused relations between text and performance. For while, in the naturalist theatre, all the elements of drama – speech, movement, design, sound – depended on the basic assumption of 'probability', all worked at least in the same general terms: if not in a single and controlled design, at least in an imposed and realizable unity. But when the element of speech began to be conceived on a different basis, this temporary stability was lost, and the total situation, in several ways, was now worse than before. In Eliot's *The Cocktail Party*, where the theme is very similar to that of *The Family Reunion*, the local difficulties of chorus and apparition were carefully avoided, but the style of the action was again 'behaviour', and the elements of movement, sound and design were frankly naturalist. Only the verse element remained, as witness to a different dramatic intention, but there was an inherent difficulty, when all other elements enforced 'probability', in performing so frankly conventional a speech. The result was what one would expect: the verse, in performance, was 'toned down', until at times it did not function as dramatic rhythm at all. And this was not, one has to insist, a problem of performance; it was a problem of dramatic conception and writing. For the text of *The Family Reunion* or *The Cocktail Party* is as essentially incomplete as the text of *The Seagull*. Many modern naturalist plays are so cluttered with italicized direction and comment that the 'clean lines' of Eliot's plays might seem a welcome improvement. But the 'cleanness' was not a solution of the problem which the italicized comments pointed towards; it was, rather, an evasion. For, in performance, not only does the speech not stand alone; all the elements of movement, sound and design are necessarily added, and, though unprescribed, radically affect the total experience of the play. But also the speech itself cannot be wholly played as written, and then the only actualized dramatic form has disintegrated.

It is then clear that dramatic verse can only be fully performed if dramatic movement and scene are in the same dimension. Otherwise, the actor has to try to follow several rhythms at once, or to move, uneasily, from one kind of representation, and one kind of reality, to another. But this movement, this relation and settling of rhythms, is the dramatist's responsibility. If he does not accept it, it is now clear that writing verse is no solution: even some very fine verse, as Eliot indeed wrote. For what he is leaving the performers to do is the reintegration of those dramatic elements, one of which he has radically altered. The actors will, as they can, speak the verse with their voices, but everything else that they are doing will come not from the *process* of the verse, but from its *product*. It is indeed this forcing of performance towards the product of dramatic writing – the detailed process of performance having been separated from that detailed process of writing which is not only the dialogue but the whole dramatic conception – which comes through as a common problem in the naturalist drama and in its apparent alternatives.

### *The Life of Galileo* by Bertolt Brecht; 1939–47

In the period in which Eliot was writing *The Family Reunion*, Bertolt Brecht was attempting a more radical dramatic reform. *The Life of Galileo* was first written in 1938 and 1939, and was revised in the years 1945–7. It was first produced at the Zürich Schauspielhaus on 9 September 1943.

*The Life of Galileo* is written in fifteen scenes. From the beginning of his dramatic conception, Brecht emphasizes a mobile and open action. This moves through a wide variety of places, but the action is created in them, by its own logic and momentum, rather than being in any way fixed. As Brecht noted:

> The stage decor must not be such that the public believes itself to be in a room in medieval Italy or in the Vatican. The public must remain always clearly aware that it is in a theatre.

The painted background should express what Brecht calls 'the historical ambience', rather than 'immediate surroundings'. It should be two-dimensional, to emphasize the contrasting plasticity of the actors. The furniture, properties and costumes within this set should be 'realistic (including doors) and, particularly, should have social-historical charm'.

The open and mobile action is in many ways a return to the theatrical methods of earlier drama, and in particular the Elizabethan. At the same time, there is an emphasis on a kind of acting and a kind of historical presence which belongs to the modern theatre, and this is again modified by Brecht's most characteristic element: that of critical presentation, rather than simple theatrical illusion – one means to this is the brief and pointed introduction, in verse, to the action and meaning of each scene. To combine and control these varying emphases needed direct intervention by the producer. As Brecht again noted:

> *The Life of Galileo* can, without much adjustment of the contemporary theatrical style, be presented as a piece of historical 'ham' with a star part. A conventional production (which, however, need never consciously strike the performers as conventional, particularly

if it contains some original ideas) must nevertheless perceptibly weaken the real power of the play, without providing the audience with 'easier access'. The most important effects of the play would misfire if the 'contemporary theatre' did not make the necessary adjustment.

It is true also, of course, that this could happen to *King Lear*, but it is significant that the precise achievement of Brecht's dramatic effects – which he was always ready to alter, experimentally, in the course of production – depended on specific direction beyond the text, and was in fact most notably present when, some years later, Brecht was able to build his own permanent company, the Berliner Ensemble, with an agreed and conscious policy and methods.

*Scene One*

We can look at a critical speech from the first scene. Galileo is washing the upper part of his body, and Andrea, his housekeeper's son, takes out from behind the starcharts in the study a large wooden model of the Ptolemaic cosmic system. This is explained and shown working:

> GALILEO: And now make the sun move.
> ANDREA: That's beautiful. But we're so shut in.

Brecht has established, with a model, the starting-point of the play, but now to express the challenge to just that narrowness of view, he changes his method. Galileo throws the towel to Andrea, so that he can dry his back. While this is happening, he tells, in some seven hundred words, of the new astronomy, and its probable liberation of men's minds and of society. In this speech, explicit dramatization, as in the use of the Ptolemaic model, is replaced by verbal description and argument. Brecht writes the speech in a largely practical way, with examples from ships, the block and tackle, the new spindles, and from the new mood:

The most solemn truths are being tapped on the shoulder; what was never doubted is now in doubt.

But it is interesting that this exposition of a new world-view, though full of practical examples, is dramatized, not in its own terms (which the stage, used in this way, would clearly not permit, though on film, for example, it would be possible) but in what is in effect the naturalistic characterization of Galileo himself. This again is not in the words, but in what is happening, within this convention, while so many words are being spoken. As Brecht reports:

A few people raised objections to Laughton delivering the first-scene speech about the new astronomy with his torso bare; they said the public might be confused by hearing such intellectual utterances from a half-naked man. But just that very mixture of spiritual and physical interested Laughton. Galileo's physical pleasure, when the boy rubbed his back, was transmuted into intellectual creativeness.

The point is not, of course, one of propriety; it is the more critical point of the relation between what is being said and what is being done, as we have already seen it in Chekhov. The interpretation – 'physical pleasure' into 'intellectual creativeness' – is clearly a way of playing the part, and has important connections to later moments in the play. But the dramatic experience then being communicated is of this very individual creativeness – at its best a great historical figure; at its worst 'a piece of historical "ham" with a star part' – when the words Brecht has written, and their fundamental viewpoint on which so much of the play depends, express something radically different – that 'everything moves', that the result of the new voyages and the new cooperative methods of working is a new social consciousness, of which the new astronomy is a part. Since just this relation between individual creativity and social consciousness is the major theme of the play, in which Brecht sees Galileo as failing because he maintains the first at the expense of the second, it is of some importance that Galileo is introduced to the audience – not in the text but in the performance – with an emphasis, and an approval of the emphasis, that the play as a whole is setting out to question. This is not, at this point, a critical method, of the kind to which Brecht's writing was directed, but a sentimental method, in a familiar dimension of acting, which seems basically to follow from the fact that the social consciousness is not dramatized but is simply reported, and that emphasis then shifts to the man reporting it, around whom some kind of stage presence, if only to fill a vacuum, must be built.

This is a general difficulty in the performance of Brecht, whose dramatic method consists, with remarkable success, in the production of cases or examples for argument, but who has then to discover ways of holding the dramatic convention at that level, against a powerful tendency, from the conventional theatre, to turn the arguments into personalities. He invented many possible means of preventing this: the use of commentators and notices; the breaking of theatrical illusion by exposing its machinery; instructions to the actors to distance themselves from their parts, as if looking at what 'he' – the character – said, with a certain objectivity. Given the common understanding and discipline of a particular company, he could create this mood, by these means. But it is ironic that it has been taken for success, elsewhere in the theatre, when this precise intention, in Brecht, has been overridden, to gain not critical inspection but sympathy, not argument, but identification: a process described as 'making the plays human', 'suppressing Brecht the dogmatist and releasing Brecht the dramatist'; when what is really happening is that the production methods of one kind of drama are absorbing and working against another kind.

*Scene Fourteen*

A similar point can be briefly illustrated from the end of the play. Andrea is taking the manuscript of Galileo's 'Discorsi' across the Italian border. The frontier guards, stupidly and perfunctorily, examine his luggage, asking 'what sort of a fellow' is Aristotle. Boys are playing around the frontier post, talking about witches. Andrea gets the precious manuscript across.

The point of this scene is at once a climax and an anticlimax of the action. Galileo, by recanting, has gained time to write the important 'Discorsi'; Andrea is taking the manuscript out to publish it and add to human knowledge. It is a success, but of a particular and limited kind, indicated by the very ignorance of the frontier guards, and the superstitious talk of the boys, which the new science had been intended to change. Brecht includes all these elements, but writes the action in a neutral way – the necessary movements of searching and crossing. It is then possible to play the scene, as is often done and as is almost universally recommended in critical commentary, to emphasize the romantic element of the taking out of the manuscript, with a certain liberal consciousness of its importance as against the stupidity or indifference of ordinary people. Nor is there anything definite, in the action, to prevent this. Andrea calls back, when he has crossed, and tells the boys to learn to open their eyes, and that nobody can fly through the air on a broomstick. But this is again detached argument, against a physical scene which can very easily – by a familiar acting of the stupidity of the boys and the guards – seem to cancel it, as a hopeless ideal. In Brecht's production, the consciousness is more open and critical, but still the dramatic reality of these two ways of looking at the scene, which we are intended to recognize and compare, is more willed than achieved.

No dramatist of his generation has been more powerful and inventive than Brecht, in the creation of new conventions, new attitudes, a newly open, mobile and critical drama. But a look at these scenes, and their inherent openness (in another sense) until the right producer arrives, reminds us how precarious the new drama can be, in the old theatres.

## *Waiting for Godot* by Samuel Beckett; 1952

A recurrent problem, in modern drama, is the realization of action: of movement, intervention, change, as opposed to watching, reacting, waiting. The latter consciousness, so perfectly expressed in the trapped rooms, the inhibited conversations, of high naturalism, has been more widely supported in Western societies than its more confident, exploratory and radical alternative. The preferred dramatic method corresponds to a dominant structure of feeling.

Beckett's achievement, in *Waiting for Godot*, is the dramatization, at an extreme point, of this familiar immobility. The two tramps, Didi and Gogo, wait in each act, with a deadening repetition, for Godot to come. Near the end of each act, a boy messenger comes to say 'not today, but tomorrow'. Each act ends with this characteristic moment:

Let's go.
*They do not move.*

The only variation between the acts, in the general action, is in the travellers, Pozzo and Lucky, who appear first as master and slave, and then as the blind being led by the dumb. It is interesting that these are the dramatic tensions of high naturalism, replayed not as tensions within an apparently acceptable and represented world, but in their own terms, as dramatic images which create the form of the total experience directly, and without the offering of local probabilities.

We can look at certain characteristic scenes in performance. The tramps, who represent, metaphorically, a more general and spiritual vagrancy, outside the compulsions of time and habit, are of course primarily presented as physical tramps, with the problems of boots and food. I saw in a programme note of an English production a description of them as an interesting kind of French vagrant, and for a time, I suppose, the action could be played in that way; its elements are there, in the way the characters are established. But the very precise writing depends on another convention: a variant of what is in effect the cross-talk act of variety. It is through this, again, that the central themes have to be introduced.

Gogo is sitting on a low mound, at the side of a road, near a bare tree. Didi walks stiffly around him.

DIDI [*angrily*]: . . . I'd like to hear what you'd say if you had what I have.

GOGO: It hurts?

DIDI: Hurts! He wants to know if it hurts! [*Stooping*] Never neglect the little things of life.

GOGO: What do you expect, you always wait till the last moment.

DIDI [*musingly*]: The last moment. [*He meditates*] Hope deferred maketh the something sick, who said that?

GOGO: Why don't you help me?

DIDI: Sometimes I feel it coming all the same. Then I go all queer.

[*He takes off his hat, peers inside it, feels about inside it, shakes it, puts it on again.*]

How shall I say? Relieved and at the same time . . . [*he searches for the word*] . . . appalled. [*With emphasis*] AP-PALLED.

[*He takes off his hat again, peers inside it.*]

Funny.

[*He knocks on the crown as if to dislodge a foreign body, peers into it again, puts it on again.*]

Nothing to be done.

[*Gogo with a supreme effort succeeds in pulling off his boot. He looks inside it, feels about inside it, turns it upside down, shakes it, looks on the ground to see if anything has fallen out, finds nothing, feels inside it again, staring sightlessly before him.*]

DIDI: Well?
GOGO: Nothing.
DIDI: Show.
GOGO: There's nothing to show.


The control in this scene is remarkable. The dependence on three levels of consciousness – the physical predicament of the tramps, the cross-talk stage element (*He wants to know if it hurts*), and the intimations of a total predicament (the scriptural reminiscence of *Hope deferred*; the repetition of *appalled*, AP-PALLED) – is controlled, not only by the precision of the writing, but also by the precision of the general dramatic imagination. It is significant that every movement and gesture is precisely written, and that these, building up from ordinary activities, compose a general rhythm – the searching, in vain, in hat and boot, and the conclusion: *Show. There's nothing to show.* This, in its apparent simplicity, is an unusual kind of writing for total performance.

We can then look, by way of contrast, at a very different dramatic problem. After Pozzo and Lucky have appeared, Pozzo commands Lucky to think. It is said he can't think without his hat, and this is put on him. Pozzo jerks the rope round Lucky's neck:

POZZO: Think, pig!

> [*Pause.* LUCKY *begins to dance.*]

Pozzo goes on with a series of staccato orders, turning Lucky this way and that. He finally turns him towards the auditorium with the renewed command:

> Think!

The speech by Lucky, that follows, is a confused, fragmentary, repetitive tirade, but running through it is a thread of meaning which is one of the central experiences of the play:

> Given the existence of a personal God who loves us dearly with some exceptions for reasons unknown but time will tell . . .

The problem in performance is the maintenance of this thread through the verbal confusion:

> Given the existence as uttered forth in the public works of Puncher and Wattman of a personal God quaquaquaqua with white beard quaquaquaqua. . . .

I have heard this speech played often enough to know that the double condition – the thread of meaning and the gabbling confusion – can be communicated, though it can also be reduced to a meaningless jabber in which not the process but the product of the confusion is performed: a simple and comic shouting against the odds. This way out has been taken in one or two eminent productions, and has been combined with a similar interpretation of Beckett's directions on the reactions of the others, while Lucky is speaking. Beckett's four stages –

1. Didi and Gogo all attention, Pozzo dejected and disgusted
2. Didi and Gogo begin to protest, Pozzo's sufferings increase

3. Didi and Gogo attentive again, Pozzo more and more agitated and groaning
4. Didi and Gogo protest violently, Pozzo jumps up, pulls on the rope. General outcry. Lucky pulls on the rope, staggers, shouts his text. All throw themselves on Lucky who struggles and shouts

– can then be reduced to a general riot, in which what is projected, in the speech and in the behaviour of the others, is the external element of the stage business, the self-sufficient dramatic figures, in a way that for all its conventional difference from naturalism – the business is confused and alienated, the figures distorted – is essentially a repetition of the naturalist theatre, with its studied, overall, behavioural sketches. This takes its place with a playing of the tramps as if they were sentimental caricatures, within the same dramatic mode. An unusually precise piece of writing, of both speech and action, can then be performed in crude general effects.

Some part of this difficulty, it is true, can be found within Beckett's dramatic conception. He is using certain theatrical conventions, though for mixed and contrary purposes. But the remarkable success of the play, as a vivid dramatic invention, is greater than it ordinarily seems when, like so much experimental drama, it comes to performance in theatres and companies (and in audiences, actors and producers), which for all their willingness to make local innovations, were formed in an older structure of feeling.

# 8

## *Wild Strawberries*, by Ingmar Bergman
## 1957

### THE CONDITIONS OF PERFORMANCE

In this work by Ingmar Bergman, we have certain wholly
new relations between what have been thought of as text and
performance. The film is in one way a single recorded performance, but in another way, and more significantly, it is
in itself the dramatic production: the actual shaping of the
work. In the case of many films, we have no access to the
script which is the written form of this work, but Bergman
has published what he calls his screenplays, and discussed their
relations to his finished films.

A film begins, he says, in a 'primitive nucleus' which
'strives to achieve definite form'. If it seems strong enough,
he decides to materialize it.

Then comes something very complicated and difficult: the transformation of rhythms, moods, atmosphere, tensions, sequences, tones
and scents into words and sentences, into an understandable screenplay.

Thus far, the process is very similar to any written creation by
a dramatic author, but of course the screenplay is written
within the consciousness of a film-maker, who has in mind
not performance by others, but his own task of creating the
finished work in sight and sound. And here at once there is a
problem of expression which is also a problem of notation.

The only thing that can be satisfactorily transferred from that
original complex of rhythms and moods is the dialogue ... Written

dialogue is like a musical score, almost incomprehensible to the average person. ... One can write dialogue, but how it should be delivered, its rhythm and tempo, what is to take place between lines – all this must be omitted for practical reasons. Such a detailed script would be unreadable.

We have seen this problem in many plays; it is not intrinsic to film. It relates, deeply, to the question of conventions of acted speech, and the consequent conventions of written speech. What is different, here, is the claim of the man who creates the original work to achieve detailed and continuous control over just these vital elements of performance. It appears as a film-making problem but as such it only concentrates certain recurring problems of writing for speaking. What is new is the maker's insistence on their direct solution, by a means available in the conditions of performance. A dramatist directing his own play would have this control, but for a performance which then disappears or at best is remembered or becomes traditional. The condition here is of one fixed production or performance, which is then indefinitely repeatable.

But the problem of the dialogue is only one part of the process. There are also

montage, rhythm and the relation of one picture to another ... Here I cannot clearly give a key, as in a musical score, nor a specific idea of the tempo which determines the relationships involved.

Neither, of course, can the traditional dramatist, except again in certain conventions, though he also is working and seeing in terms which are more than sound. What he writes as scene, and all the visual elements of the action, have to be realized from indications which, in very much this way, may lack certain crucial elements of tempo and relationship, but also, of course, which is not mentioned, the detailed substance of what is particularly seen. If we think back to the problem of text and performance in Chekhov's *The Seagull*, we realize that this again is not intrinsic to film.

What is different in film, from most traditional kinds of dramatic performance, is the element of conscious assembly – the breaking into sequences, shot over weeks or months, and only rarely in any final order; the crucial work of cutting and editing. Again, as creation, this is not in general new. Writers work on their texts in this way: often writing scenes out of order; rearranging, cutting, editing. But there is a different substance to handle, when this is done in film: not the indications of a performance, but the production itself. And it is here that the problem of notation which many dramatists have been conscious of is still acute:

I have often wished for a kind of notation which would enable me to put on paper all the shades and tones of my vision, to record distinctly the inner structure of a film. For when I stand in the artistically devastating atmosphere of the studio, my hands and head full of all the trivial and irritating details that go with motion-picture production, it often takes a tremendous effort to remember how I originally saw and thought out this or that sequence, or what was the relation between the scene of four weeks ago and that of today. If I could express myself clearly, in explicit symbols, then this problem would be almost eliminated and I could work with absolute confidence that whenever I liked I could prove the relationship between the part and the whole and put my finger on the rhythm, the continuity of the film. Thus the script is a very imperfect *technical* basis for a film.

This is convincing, but it is worth remembering that in the absence of clear conventions of performance – on which any usable notation would have to be based – this is a persistent problem in all modern drama. What has happened in Bergman's case, though by no means in all films, is that the dramatic author has become his own director: the unity of text and performance is achieved, not conventionally, but in the phases of work of one mind.

When we see *Wild Strawberries*, we are in conditions in some ways comparable to those of the modern theatre – that it is on no special occasion; that it is one of a number of comparable productions among which we choose – but in other ways different – that it is often part of a continuous run of films, with people coming and going at different times and so (normally) without that conscious or self-conscious assembly at a theatre; that the darkness of the auditorium is of a different depth and quality, in which we are less conscious of other spectators; and that what we are seeing, on the variety of possible screens, has certain radically altered dimensions. The figures and images are customarily larger – often much larger – than life, and it is of course a crucial element of their composition that this degree is variable, over a very wide range, for dramatic emphasis, and that this, with other alterations such as focus, is in itself a new relationship with the audience, directing elements of response and attention in much more formal and confident ways. The whole status of 'scene' has also been transformed. We move normally, and in *Wild Strawberries* especially, not through a series of fixed dramatic scenes, but through a composition of many real and imagined landscapes, between which and the persons of the action there are powerfully variable relationships. Often, in particular shots and sequences, we recognize a clear continuity with elements of dramatic scene and spectacle, but there is also, by the controlling fact of the camera, an exceptional integration of what are thought of in traditional dramatic terms as the separable elements of characters and scenes. This fact of the camera, moreover, continually determining, not as a choice but as the only access to the work, the essential point of view on the action – the movement from here to there, the alteration of angle, the closing or distancing of a viewpoint – adds a dimension to all previously known dramatic means. There are formal precedents, within the structure of many kinds of play, but in film the spectator has been more completely integrated with this structure, while he watches it at all. The position of the spectator is then very different: he has learned the conventions of this highly mobile and flexible form, and sees *with* it, in a radical way. The element of separation between spectator and action has been drastically reduced, and very often, while we are watching a film, seems to vanish altogether, so that it is through our eyes that this movement seems directed. This condition of performance has been widely abused, in many commercial films; and the integration of critical faculty with this kind of seeing, though wholly possible, is in many ways harder than when the separation has more evidently supporting physical conditions. At the same time, the degree of control given to the maker of the work, in conjunction with the powerful nature of the medium itself, provides real conditions for important dramatic art. In fact, since film production reached its maturity, in the second and third decades of the twentieth century, its contributions to the whole body of drama have at least equalled, and in my view clearly surpassed, the contributions of the theatre in the same period.

We are watching *Wild Strawberries*, then: written and filmed in Sweden. A voice is speaking to us, through and over the images we are seeing.

## THE SCREENPLAY

The controlling form of *Wild Strawberries* is that of the first-person narrative, in which we at once see the retired professor, Isak Borg, and hear him giving an account of his life. This is a choice related to the substance of the experience, which is retrospective and reflecting but also, quite formally, an accounting, a coming to account. He is telling the story of a single day, in which he travels to the University of Lund to become a 'jubilee doctor', but through the events of the day he is expressing his own fears and loneliness, looking back at some critical early experiences, of a haunting kind (which now, through the conventions of the film, and of the directing camera, can be seen, rather than simply recalled), and finally coming to terms with his relationships and with himself.

Two general points can then be made about the dramatic form. First, that it evidently relates to some previous forms, in both drama and the novel: to the retrospective calling-to-account of Ibsen's *Masterbuilder* or *John Gabriel Borkman*, and more particularly to the journey of discovery between present and past in Strindberg's *To Damascus*; and also to the first-person narrative novel, in which there is both account and recreation, as in Henry James's *Turn of the Screw* or Thomas Mann's *Felix Krull* or many other and varied works. Second, that the forms available, in those plays and novels, have been extended, and in important ways strengthened, through the availability of particular techniques. Thus there is a newly available simultaneity of reflective account and remembered scene, in an active presence and tension, because film has made it possible both to play or replay the scene and to have the exploring voice through and over it: a simultaneous involvement and distancing, as repeatedly in *Wild Strawberries*, when there can be a shift back in time, to the experience of a child or young man, and yet the voice and appearance of the man involved in this reliving are of the present: of age and separation. Further, much of this characteristic experience is of dream as much as of memory, of vision and fantasy as much as of recollection and accounting, and the movement between these states of being is much more flexible than in forms which can create one or the other, but usually at best in alternation, more commonly in the determination of the whole form by a selected single state; and while not more flexible than fictional narrative, has more immediate opportunities for realization – for detailed seeing, and for an objective seeing which can interact with the spoken consciousness. What has then often been achieved by separate techniques is here more immediately available as a total form. This is not to say that *Wild Strawberries* as a particular work is more powerful than the other examples I have mentioned; indeed it quite clearly is not. But the form available to the artist, for this characteristic experience, is unusually integrated and powerful.

The problem of writing for film is also, as it happens, much simpler in this method and experience. For the narrator can describe, in detail, in ways that would be very difficult in dialogue: he can describe the dress and appearance of the people he sees and meets; or the configuration of a nightmare which could not come to dialogue at all; or the details of significant objects – the setting of the dining-room, the doll, the lecture theatre and the microscope. Thus what the narrator is saying is a direction to see, as in a novelist's description, but also – though not always – a direction to the director, to what will be seen in the film. In other methods and experiences, as in some of Bergman's other screenplays, the problem of writing for film is much more intractable; the dramatic convention beyond speech has few precedents and is very much harder to achieve.

The text of the screenplay of *Wild Strawberries* is some fourteen thousand words. It is of course not divided into acts; the scenes are in sequence, and were numbered. The running time of the film is ninety minutes.

## The Dream in the Car

We can take for detailed examination parts of an eighteen-minute sequence, about two thirds of the way through the film. Borg, in the car, falls asleep and dreams. In the screenplay he has described 'the dark gleaming surface of Lake Vättern', the 'thin jagged scratches of summer lightning', 'the breeze' and the 'approaching storm'.

I fell asleep . . . I was pursued by dreams and images which seemed extremely real and were very humiliating to me.

The sequence opens with Borg speaking these words. There is the sound of a guitar, being played by one of the young passengers, and through it the sound of thunder. There is a long shot of the surface of the lake, and then, ahead through the rain-blurred windscreen, of the road seen past the moving wiper. There are middle-distance shots of the passengers, and of Borg and Marianne in front. Then a sudden close-up of Borg's head is succeeded by a sharp noisy flight of rooks: the moment of the beginning of the dream. This is succeeded by a close-up of the basket of wild strawberries, and the camera moves back to show us Borg, at his present age, with his former girl-friend Sara, young as in his memory. The speech between them is played as written, with conventional angles and cutting: Sara over Borg's shoulder; Borg over Sara's shoulder, alternately. Sara forces him to look in the mirror: he is 'a worried old man who will die soon' while she is a girl with her 'whole life' before her. Because he is old and knows nothing, she will marry his brother Sigfrid.

The relationship, in this way, is very quickly established, not by the dream-technique of obvious distortion, but by the juxtaposition of different phases of time, which can then be played as if real. The Sara of the dream is also the unrelated Sara to whom they have given a lift. The figure within the consciousness, in this painful memory, can be played in real terms, with an unusual flexibility. Sara's use of the mirror is a way of forcing Borg to look at himself; he is reluctant and draws back, and when she says he is smiling it is no more than the reflected light of the mirror, moving on his face.

In the screenplay, Sara then throws away the mirror and it breaks. There is the sound of wind and of a child crying. In the film, Sara runs through the garden to the cradle. In the screenplay, the cradle is in an arbour, but in the film it is a white blowing frame of muslin under the dark branches of a tree. The music rises as she runs, and then, quietly, in a held medium shot, Sara speaks to the baby: '... don't be afraid of the birds ...'. The voice direction in the screenplay – 'half singing ... very distant and sorrowful' – is replaced by a sad, still voice: its normality accentuated. She does not, as in the screenplay, cry, but even smiles at the end. There is a further long shot of her crossing the garden to the house; there are shadows and the sound of wind, as in the beginning of the dream. We see, as in the screenplay, Sigfrid waiting and taking her into the house.

In the screenplay, Borg says: 'I wanted to scream until my lungs were bloody'. In the film this becomes a sequence in which Borg, in his turn, goes to the cradle; this is preceded, as before, by the flight of birds, and the sound of their cries. He stands over the white blowing cradle, with the dark jagged branches heavily shadowed behind his head. We see him in close-up, looking away and with the sea beyond; then the branches in close-up; then a view of Borg from behind, in which the screen is momentarily black and then clears into a shape as the shoulders of his coat. He moves up to the house.

The relation between text and performance, in this first sequence, is close but in many ways indirect. All the essential images, with the exception of the branches, were written, but are then, in performance, rearranged. A narrative sequence in the writing is replaced by a sharper dramatic sequence in the filming: the juxtaposition of images, rather than the general description. The written speech, between the characters, is played directly and closely, following the screenplay.

What is involved in the sequence we have looked at is partly 'atmosphere', of a kind very similar to Stanislavsky's directions for Chekhov, but the medium makes its integration more direct, in a way of seeing which is continuous with the character of Borg. The sequence that follows is different in that the film moves to an objective viewpoint, in which we see Borg, his situation and his memories, from a cool distance. This change of emphasis, within the dream convention, is very simply achieved. After Borg has looked in at Sara and Sigfrid, as at a lighted stage-set, with flowers, music and wine, he turns and looks up at the moon and its shadows. Then he turns again to what seems to be the same door, and another face appears: Alman, whom he had met on the road, and who seems now to be his examiner. This is a sharper transition than in the screenplay, where a voice calls his name and he 'turns and recognizes' Alman. The exact sequence is as follows:

1. Close-up: Alman's face through the glass. The door is opening. ALMAN: Come in.
2. Medium: Borg goes in.
3. Long: Borg and Alman, walking through two bare rooms, one with a stair.
4. Medium: In a third room, Alman opens a door. Borg goes through first.
5. Long: Corridor, white boards, black and white walls.
6. Medium: Alman unlocks door.
7. Close-up: Borg looks inside.
8. Medium: Lecture theatre. Four people in desks.
9. Close-up: Borg.
10. Medium: Blackboard, with a strange message written on it, desk in front; Alman sits.
    ALMAN: Do you have your examination book with you?
11. Medium: Borg produces the book. BORG: Here it is.

12. Medium: ALMAN: Thank you. (He looks quickly through the book.) ALMAN: Will you please identify the bacteriological specimen in the microscope? Take your time.

13. Close-up: Borg at microscope.

14. Close-up: An enlarged eye.

15. Close-up: Borg disturbed. BORG: There must be something wrong with the microscope.

16. Medium: Alman and Borg. Alman looks in microscope.

17. Medium: ALMAN: There's nothing wrong with the microscope.
    BORG: I can't see anything.
    ALMAN: Sit down.

18. Medium: ALMAN: Will you please read this text?

19. Close-up: BORG: Inke tan magrov stak farsin los kret fajne kaserte mjotron presete.

20. Close up: ALMAN: What does it mean?

21. Close-up: BORG: I don't know.

22. Close-up: ALMAN: Really?

23. Close-up: BORG: I'm a doctor, not a linguist.

24. Close-up: ALMAN: Then let me tell you, Professor Borg, that on the blackboard is written the first duty of a doctor.

25. Close-up: Borg.

26. Close-up: ALMAN: Do you happen to know what that is?

27. Close-up: BORG: Yes, if you let me think for a moment.
    ALMAN'S VOICE: Take your time.
    BORG: A doctor's first duty ... a doctor's first duty ... a doctor's ... I've forgotten.

28. Close-up: Borg.

29. Close-up: ALMAN: A doctor's first duty is to ask forgiveness.

30. Close-up: Borg, laughs.

31. Long: Borg turns and looks at auditorium.

This is, throughout, very close to the screenplay, with only slight changes of detail. The strangeness of the eye in the microscope and the meaningless words on the board is held, throughout, within an enforced normality of speech and action, pointed only by the tension of the rapid alternation of the two speaking figures.

Where the screenplay has been realized in dialogue, within an objective situation, the filming is indeed its direct performance. The greater difficulties arise when the atmosphere of a scene is still connected with Borg's consciousness, by narrative, and yet has to emerge in something like its own right. The next important sequence, in which Borg sees his wife and her lover, is a good example. In the screenplay there is a long verbal description of moving through the woods; in the film this is replaced by visual composition, of water and shadows and trees – the visual images, as it happens, are less precise than those that had been written. The memory, as in the scene of Sara and Sigfrid, is visually established in a frame: there the look through the window, here a long shot through the dark wood into a lighted clearing. The essential action is then as written, but in a different dimension of composition: the figure of the wife, at least, emerges from the narrative memory and takes over as a direct character, even before her final written speech. The main advantage, in this sequence, of the film as a method is that, with camera movement and cutting, the scene can be both direct and observed, where a theatre dramatist, normally, would have to choose between viewpoints, or more obviously move between one and the other. Here the scene in the clearing is dominant, but there is a continual rapid cutting to Borg's face, watching, behind a frame of branches, and the action and the memory are thus both simultaneous and distinct.

We can see this in the wife's last speech. I set it down, as written, and with the actual filmed sequence, in italics.

{ WOMAN: He'll say: you shouldn't ask forgiveness from me.
    [*Medium: Woman leaning forward, gazing in mirror.*]
{ [*Close-up*]: Borg's face
    WOMAN: I have nothing to forgive.
    [*Close-up: Woman's face.*]
    WOMAN: But he doesn't mean it, because he's as cold as
    ice. . . . He'll say that he'll bring me a sedative and that
    he understands everything. And then I'll say
{ [*Close-up: Borg.*]
    WOMAN: That it's his fault I'm the way I am, and he'll
    look very sad and say
{ [*Close-up: Woman.*]
    WOMAN: That it's his fault. But he doesn't care about
    anything, because he's completely cold.

This shows very clearly a new dramatic method, in the use
of voice and face, where by the choice of image, and by
cutting, a significantly altered relation between who is speaking and who is being referred to, between accusation from
another and silent accusation of oneself, can be directly composed. *Wild Strawberries* is not, in dramatic material, very
different from the theatre plays from which, in important
respects, it derives, but much of the experience written with
difficulty for the theatre can now be directly and powerfully
performed.

# 9

# Argument: Text and Performance

THE word *drama* is used in two main ways: first, to describe a literary work, the text of a play; and, second, to describe the performance of this work, its production. Thus, the text of *King Lear* is drama, and Shakespeare, as a writer, a dramatist; while a performance of *King Lear* is also drama, its players engaged in a dramatic activity. The acts of writing a play and of performing it are clearly distinct, as are the experiences of reading a play and of watching its performance, yet the word *drama* is equally meaningful when applied to either. Nor is the coincidence of the word accidental: for drama, as a literary form, is a work intended for performance, and, similarly, the great majority of performances are of literary works. It is true that we find, at one extreme, works which are cast in a dramatic form, but which are now very difficult or impossible to perform, and are therefore mainly known to us through reading; and again, at the other extreme, we find some performances which are not based on any written work, or on any complete written work, or which, if so based, are not accompanied by publication, so that we can know the work only in performance. These extremes are both drama; but the normal situation is that there is a work of literature, the play, which is intended to be performed, but can also be read, and which, in either case, we shall properly recognize as drama.

When a dramatist writes a play, he is not writing a story which others can adapt for performance: he is writing a literary work in such a manner that it can be directly performed.

## DRAMATIC ACTION

Drama can be further defined as *action*, which is the meaning of the original Greek word δρᾶμα. *Action*, as a definition, can usefully indicate the method of the literary form, or the process of the theatrical performance. It must not be used, however, as if it were equivalent to a certain kind of performance, or a certain kind of dramatic substance. *Action* refers to the nature of the literary conception; to the method of the literary work; and to the manner of its communication. Further, because of the great variety of the dramatic tradition, it refers, at different times and in different places, to methods which differ, and which have to be distinguished. On the basis of the performances that have been considered, we can distinguish four kinds of dramatic action:

(*a*) *Acted Speech:* the kind of action found in the *Antigone*, in the medieval plays, and in parts of the Elizabethan drama. Here, the drama is conceived, and the literary work is written, in such a way that when, in the known conditions of performance, the words are enacted, the whole of the drama is thereby communicated. Further, the literary form – the detailed arrangement of the words – prescribes, in the known conditions, the exact action. There is no important action that is separate from the words – 'the poetry is the action'. The action is a necessary unity of speech and movement – 'acted speech'; and where there are minor actions that are separate, these again are prescribed by the form as a whole, which is fully realized in the words, written for known performance conditions.

(*b*) *Visual Enactment:* the kind of action developed from the separate minor actions of the previous form. Here, an action exactly prescribed by the literary form, but not directly accompanied by speech, is separately performed. When a

performer enacts an emotion, in response to the speech of
*another*, the beginnings of this method are evident. It is taken
further, as in the final ascent of Everyman, when an action is
made *necessary* by the speech of another. Finally, a situation
that has already been defined in speech may be separately
enacted, without speech, as in the duel of Hamlet and Laertes;
or may be separately enacted, to the accompaniment of the
speech of a *narrator*; or, in the simplest example, may (as in the
early Elizabethan dumb-show) precede the full performance.
This kind of action has been separately developed, as in various
forms of dance-drama, and of ballet: in Yeats's *At the Hawk's
Well*, the form of the hawk's dance is prescribed by the literary
work, but the detail is determined by the actual dancer; in
ballet, the separate enactment has become a whole art, and
does not directly depend on a literary work.

(*c*) *Activity*: the kind of action, as in *The Feast at Solhoug*,
which, in our time, is often thought to be the *only* kind of
dramatic action. Here, there is no direct unity of speech and
movement; but the movement, usually arranged in a pattern
of exciting events, is primary, and the dramatic speech exists
mainly to give the cue for these events, to explain them, and
to punctuate them by simple cries of alarm, warning, shock
and so on. It is not a verbal design being communicated in a
whole action, but a series of events being intermittently
accompanied by words.

(*d*) *Behaviour*: the kind of action, as in *The Seagull*, where the
words and movement have no direct and necessary relation,
but derive, as it were separately, from a conception of 'probable behaviour'in the circumstances presented. Words and
movements often equally communicate the dramatic experience, but not in a design of 'acted speech'; the speech, as
we have seen in the performance of *The Seagull*, is often
separate from the 'acting'. The speech is prescribed, but the

'acting', and 'setting', and therefore the action as a whole, must often be separately inferred, even where the conditions of performance are known.

The distinction of these four kinds of *action* is, it will be noted, based largely on matters of emphasis. We often find a single play containing action of more than one type, but the range nevertheless remains clear. It is in these terms that we can understand the essential difference between, say, the *Antigone* and *The Seagull*, although both are works of dramatic literature. It is in these terms, also, that the varying relation between text and performance in drama must be understood.

## THE RELATION OF TEXT AND PERFORMANCE

Drama is commonly made of four elements: *speech* (in its most general sense, including, at times, singing and recitative, as well as dialogue and conversation); *movement* (including gesture, dance, physical enactment, and acted event); *design* (including scene, scenery, costume and effects of lighting); and *sound* (as distinct from the use of the human voice – e.g. music, 'sound effects'). All these elements can appear in performance; what is variable is their relation to the literary work, the text. For example, in the categories of action already distinguished:

(*a*) *Acted Speech:* when a text of this kind – e.g. the *Antigone* – is set in the known conditions of performance for which the dramatist was writing, the full detail of the performance is seen to be prescribed. Speech and movement are determined by the arrangement of the words, according to the known conventions; design and sound are again conventional, known to the dramatist from the conditions of performance, and controlled by him in these terms. In such a case, the dramatist is not only writing a literary work; he is also, by the use of exact conventions, *writing the performance*. Performance, here, is a physical communication of a work that is, in its text, dramatically complete.

(*b*) *Visual Enactment:* here the relation of text and performance will vary according to the degree of convention of what is to be visually enacted. Where this is fully conventional (a precisely known action or pattern of movements) the text exactly prescribes the performance, by stage direction, or by necessary inference from the verbal design. In other cases, the text does no more than prescribe an *effect*, of which the *means* must be worked out in performance.

(*c*) *Activity:* here, although the text may in a general way prescribe the action, the effect of the performance will usually be very different from the effect of the text alone. The physical action will take charge, and the words will be subordinate to it. It is unusual for a dramatist writing a play of this type to realize, in his own work, the full dramatic movement; and there will usually be scope for considerable variation in performance; especially since the movements will normally be a representation of events, detailed means of which will be usually left to performance.

(*d*) *Behaviour:* here we find the widest separation between text and performance. The prescribed dramatic speech is 'probable conversation', and because in this there can be no exact relation between the arrangement of words and the method of speaking them, the performance will inevitably be an 'interpretation' of the text, and hence subject to wide variation. Movement and scene will be described in general terms, of which the detail is left to performance; but because they are understood as 'probable behaviour' and 'probable setting', they will be subject to further variations of interpretation. Indeed, the performance of a text of this kind is based less on the text than on a *response to the text*. This type, in fact, is often nearer to 'a story which others adapt for performance' than to the text which has only to be communicated to be fully performed.

On the basis of these distinctions, it is evident that there is no constant relation between text and performance in drama. Moreover, the variations have always to be understood in terms of changing methods of dramatic writing and playing. As a matter of theory, the variations have to be recognized; we must always clarify the alternative areas of fact. Because, in our own time, the normal types of dramatic action are 'activity' and 'behaviour', the necessary separation of text and performance has often been taken for granted, and, as a consequence, a separation has been assumed between literature and theatre. The separation is real, in much of our own drama; but we must not allow ourselves to be persuaded that it is inherent in all drama. At first, we can say that 'here it is so, and there not so', and this is important, as a counter to dogma. But then, inevitably, we must go on to express preferences between the alternatives. We must make, not only the theoretical recognition, but also a practical criticism; and, in this, the emphasis will tend to fall on the dramatic problems of our own day.

### ACTION AND REALITY

We have been looking at methods of writing and methods of performance. These methods acquire, at a certain point, a material reality: most notably in the structures of theatres, but also in forms of texts. Any reality inherited in this way sets certain limits, indicates certain bearings, for the making of drama. Without this inheritance, the drama could not work at all, but in periods of change the restrictions can be very obvious. In fact, during the last hundred years, most serious dramatists have complained of these restrictions, and many of them have been in active revolt against what seemed a settled and frustrating establishment. Out of the energy of this revolt, most of the important new work has come.

Yet we must not put our whole emphasis on this revolt against established structures and conventions. For if we do, we are describing it in too negative a way. The only positive description we shall be left with is an unfocused, an imprecise, creative energy. What has always to be emphasized is the profound relation between methods of writing and performance and particular views of reality. In each generation, the old methods are called conventional, but in an art like the drama the successful new method is in itself a convention. The writing and performance of drama depends on that kind of agreement – it need not altogether be prior agreement; it can be reached in the act itself – on the nature of the action being presented. What is called conventional, in the sense of an old routine, is a method or set of methods which presents a different kind of action, and through it a different kind of reality.

An audience is always the most decisive inheritance, in any art. It is the way in which people have learned to see and respond that creates the first essential condition for drama. Thus we often take for granted that any audience will understand the highly conventional nature of any dramatic performance: that the action inhabits its own dimension, and is in that sense different from other kinds of action. Yet it is not only that in some other societies, where there is no effective dramatic tradition, we find that this very particular response – depending on very intricate assumptions, adjustments and restraints, as is obvious when it has to be stated theoretically – can fail to be made. It is also that even in societies with an effective and widespread dramatic tradition, there is great practical variation in the response itself. It is obvious, for example, in our own society, that there is great uncertainty about the reality, and the implications for reality, of certain kinds of dramatic action, and about the criteria, the references, by which the reality of any particular play should be judged. This uncertainty has been much more evident since drama became a true majority form, especially on television. It is easy to respond to this, and to the kinds of complaint it continually generates, with an apparent sophistication, derived from a particular and learned distinction between art and reality: 'it is only, after all, a play', or 'we are not so naïve as to expect a play to reproduce reality exactly'. But this is not much more than a class habit. The responses being argued, the references being made, often in very confused local ways, seem to any historian of the drama the permanent and essential and very difficult questions, with which the long history of the art has always been directly concerned.

The relation between a dramatic action and reality, that is to say, is not to be settled by a formula: by the effective dramatic methods, the conventions, of a particular period. Dramatic actions at once express and test the many versions of reality which are possible, and it is in the end a more serious response to a play to complain that a character 'should not have behaved like that' – since the relation between the action and the reality is then being actively weighed – than to retreat from such questions into some notion of aesthetic propriety, which in ruling out such a question would rule out also the major dramatic interests of the whole European tradition.

When the argument can be seen as an argument about convention, there is a possibility of moving on from what is often an angry and very local confusion. But then to see the problem as one of convention is only to raise, in a more open way, very similar questions about dramatic action and its relation to reality. For a convention is not just a method: an arbitrary and voluntary technical choice. It embodies in itself those emphases, omissions, valuations, interests, indifferences, which compose a way of seeing life, and drama as part of life. Certainly we have to insist that the masked actors and chorus in the Theatre of Dionysus at Athens were not less real than the costumed actors on the furnished set of *Caste* at the Prince of Wales's Theatre, London. But we have then also to recognize that the reality, in each case, depends on a whole set of other interests, responses and assumptions; in fact on that selection of interests and values that we call a particular culture.

This point bears both ways. It is useful as a defence against rigid assumptions, about the 'true nature' of drama, or 'effective theatre', in any particular period. As we have seen, the real range of dramatic method, in writing and in performance, is immense. But this does not mean that the whole of this range is available to anyone wishing to use it. On the contrary, a method can be effectively rooted in experience only when it connects with ways of seeing and responding that are more than 'methods'; when it connects with real interests and possible ways of seeing.

One lesson that we then have to draw is that some of the major drama of the past, which we can see to be superbly fashioned for its own purposes, is, while always available as art (the art of another period, to be consciously looked at) not at all available, in the same way, as a basis for new work. In practice, always, an apparent use of some older dramatic method is a substantial change of it, in a new context. Where it is simply transplanted (as in Eliot's drawing-room Eumenides) it is neither old nor new, and no effective convention is discoverable. And where, as has happened, an older method is wholly reworked – as in Brecht's reworking of direct address, from what had become localized as exposition, soliloquy and aside – it begins to operate in a new structure of feeling, and to have quite different implications and effects.

The magnificent design of a play like Sophocles' *Antigone* depends, that is to say, on an idea of design which is no longer generally dramatically available. The same is true of *Everyman*, where the willingness to see and respond in that way is a critical feature of the success of the method. Such ideas of design are widely variable, as is already obvious between the *Antigone* and *Everyman*. The essential design of *Antony and Cleopatra* – its responses to space and power, to love and death – is similarly particular. And I think we have to go on to recognize that 'design', in these senses, is radically different from 'representation', in its modern senses. There is a critical and revolutionary change from dramatic production of a design to the dramatic reproduction of a different and more locally human order of experience. The naturalist revolution has been very long; some of its elements appear, already, in the transition from medieval to Elizabethan drama. But it was only when it was almost complete that we could see its full implications, which were basically that human experience can be understood in solely human terms, and that what has to be dramatized is this human action, however local it may seem, rather than the setting of this human action in a version of divine or cosmic reality.

Certain essential changes of convention were made necessary by this new emphasis. These were part of the major and irreversible change from feudal to bourgeois societies: a movement away from intrinsic design, hierarchy, and a perspective that reached beyond man. But the bourgeois revolt was itself very complicated. At one obvious level, which seems to culminate in *Caste* and its innumerable successors, the emphasis was on man wholly visible in society, which then allowed a method of dramatic representation, almost literally reproduction, that had its own internal consistencies but also, obviously, its limits. Within this movement, and eventually declaring itself as its enemy, was an emphasis on man, on his private and social experience, which was simultaneously an emphasis on his complexity, on his lack of transparency, and so on the inadequacy of his ordinary external representations. This is the basis of the distinction we have already made between 'the naturalist habit' and 'naturalism', but it is also the basis of a very important connection between naturalism, in this full sense, and its successors, in turn its enemies, which, in expressionism, symbolism and the absurd, created methods which directly rather than indirectly dramatized the complex, the opaque and the internal experience.

This connection further allows us to see a point of great significance in any contemporary consideration of dramatic action: that these later experimental forms shared with high naturalism an unusual fixity and stasis, for which, in the naturalist habit (from the indicated pictures of *The London Merchant* to the picture-frame stage of *Caste*) the theatres were already prepared. The structure of the *Antigone*, it is true, had been built on moments of achieved stasis: the indications, the sculptured scenes, that we noted. But there the design, in the open theatre as in the detailed experience of the writing, referred the audience outwards, to an accessible order. The simpler *Everyman* could build this order, with God on his scaffold, as the dramatic locale. It was only in *Antony and Cleopatra*, and, significantly, in the whole drama of that period, that movement itself, the direct dramatization of historical action, could be made the basis of a dramatic method. And this is above all an action in which men are making their immediate history, rather than reacting to a history which is determined or being made outside them. But in the deadlock of high naturalism, and in the enclosed, static actions of the counter-naturalist forms which suceeded it, there has been, especially in the theatre, a progressive immobility, in most serious work. The stasis of *Waiting for Godot* is in that sense a true culmination. The first form of this stasis was the stage as a room: not just the triumph of theatrical carpentry, but the conviction that important reality occurred in rooms – the rooms of private houses – to which report was carried, from which people looked and went out, but where the central interest – what was called 'what happened, not to society, but to people' – was played through. Experiment, within naturalism, was then largely a series of indications, by atmosphere, visual devices, descriptions, insets, of what went on and what existed, beyond both the room and the stage. The second form of this stasis was indeed a clearing of the room from the stage, but its replacement by the drama of a single mind, in which, so to say, those men staring from the windows of a naturalist room, feeling trapped and baffled as they looked out at the world, were replaced by a dramatic form in which the stare from the window was the essential viewpoint on reality, and what was seen, in the action, was one man's version of his world, within which he created figures to enact it.

What is then interesting is that the film and television camera, which so radically extended the possible range of dramatic methods, could be used for any of these underlying conventions. They could look into the room, with greater subtlety of detail in this face, this hand, this object, and they could solve, technically, many of the problems of inset, extension, visual device. In a majority of cases, they have done no more; the essential conventions are still of the stage as a room, with some mechanically extending movements beyond it. Or, in a different convention, the camera could be, more powerfully than on the stages of expressionism, symbolism and the absurd, a watching and shaping eye, which made a version of the world, and composed figures within it. These seem, now, the serious uses, but we have to remember how deep was that element of the high bourgeois drama in which reaction rather than action was selected for emphasis. It is one thing to react when there is an order to react to: as in the quite different dramatic designs of Greek, medieval, neo-classical and some Renaissance drama. It is quite another matter, in our kind of world, to exclude decisive action – direct intervention, open conflict, the acts of building and destroying – from the dramatic version of reality as a whole.

The mind seems to move, at this point. For it is of course true that in part of the dramatic tradition, from the duel in *Hamlet* to the poisoning at Solhoug and its many equivalents and successors, action, of an apparently direct kind, has been constantly dramatized and has been popular. What we have to ask, I think, is why that sort of action has been so commonly relegated to the less serious levels of drama: 'blood-and-thunder', 'epic', 'all action and no experience'. It is true that most of it has been self-sufficient and enclosed. The fight or the chase comes up with a predictability, at certain points in the action, which makes certain that however we respond to it at the time we have usually not seen or learned anything that we would want to remember: that no dramatic experience, in the full sense, as opposed to a temporarily exciting activity, has been created. But it does not follow that the mere exclusion of that kind of action – and so the resolution of all conflicts within the room or within the mind – is any greater guarantee of dramatic seriousness. The assumption that it is so has more to do with certain habits of our culture than with the intrinsic possibilities of drama. What seems to matter, as we begin to look at it in this way, is why that kind of action was separated from serious dramatic experience, until to go beyond the room, or beyond the observing mind, was not to go into the streets, the workplaces, the assemblies, but into what seemed merely noisy, busy and external. In the popular drama, we have stayed with the dramatization of crime, of historical actions, of adventure and exploration: significantly often in other places and other times, from the costume epic to the Western, but often, also, in our own places and times, where the action is visible and where it can be said to be, as in that regular metaphor, dramatic.

## ACTION AND WRITING

The problem of the theatre returns to haunt us. For it is the equation of drama with theatre that is now our most evident difficulty. In many theatres of the past, action of the most open kind could be written and played. But steadily, the walls were built: around the action, and around the whole performance. A moving and open art became relatively static and framed, and a quite different 'art of the theatre' was developed within these voluntary limits. A division occurred, between writing and action, which has become more apparent in each successive phase of this culture. One of the sources of this division was print: the attachment of writing to this static form, away from the human voices and movements to which it stood in a merely abstract relation. Another source, of a deeper kind, was a revaluation of action within the society. Certain 'representative' modes of dramatic writing seem to have developed, hand in hand, with certain 'representative' institutions for political action and decision. Near their most serious interests, most men learned to give up the idea of intervention, participation, direct action, even as a possibility, in favour of indirect, conventional and reacting forms. The desire for action was not lost, but was specialized to certain areas, away from central concerns. It seems paradoxical to say that the drama has lost the secret of action when Drury Lane, in the nineteenth century, could put on its stage a huge tank for a naval battle or lines for a train crash, or when commercial television, in our own period, shows every night, in careful detail, a bank robbery, a murder, a fight between spies, a running battle across a plain. But the truth is that *these* things can be enacted, because they belong in the margins of the society and the mind. Other things can be discussed, reacted to, but only rarely shown. In particular, any decisive action, in which men in general try to change their condition, is unconsciously ruled out. The social like the spiritual crisis is resolved by adjustment, in which the world can be rearranged in the mind, or presented in a singular distortion, but not, in the dramatic action, fully engaged with, struggled against, altered. This deep lack in the society has been the source of the dramatic crisis as of so much else. Our enclosed theatres, in which the acts of adjustment grow constantly in re-finement, can be seen as its temples. Film and television, inherently more open and active forms, repeated this essential process, in a majority of cases: whether as marginal spectacle or as enclosed adjustment. Briefly, in the Romantic drama, after the French Revolution, action was forced back into dramatic writing, but this drama never found its adequate theatre. In our own time, as in some parts of the world some deadlocks have been broken, the cinema has dramatized direct action, not just as spectacle – the Drury Lane tank swollen to a giant set – but as contemporary reality, in which men move and decide, on their most serious experiences. Here, undoubtedly, is the point of growth of any drama of our century: to go where reality is being formed, at work, in the streets, in assemblies, and to engage at those points with the human needs to which the actions relate.

## WRITING A DRAMATIC ACTION

Drama is always so central an element of the life of a society that a change in its methods cannot be isolated from much wider changes. While people's feelings, essentially, are shut up in rooms, the drama will stay with them. While action is only interesting, because distanced and uninvolving, in crime and sensation or in distant places and times, the majority forms will go on serving those interests. While society is generalized, and separated from the life of the individual, drama will pursue contemporary reality not as a human need but as a general report, as in the rise of documentary as a method. The important changes will come together or not at all, but this is not to say that they will all come at once, in some sudden transformation. They will come here and there, as possible new actions and methods.

And it is then worth considering the problems of the dramatist, in this kind of change. At a certain point, as we have seen, dramatists stopped writing actions, in any whole sense, and either wrote a pattern of response, which the new arts of stage-management, naturalist acting and production built into a performance, or sketched a general action – what is still sometimes called a scenario – which they would punctuate with directions, exclamations and the necessary minimum of information, the real action being staged by someone other than the writer, usually the spectacular producer or director. Plays became scripts: stories which others adapted for performance, whether of a naturalist or spectacular kind. And this convention, now, has been deeply learned; it is what is asked for; what writers exist to provide.

In the enclosed conditions of the theatres, a dramatist who goes in and learns the accepted rules can write a work which goes with the grain, and is in that sense complete. But the major difficulty is still that these rules are not just the facts of performance; they are the expression of a particular structure of feeling, a set of interests, valuations and indifferences. In some ways this is now breaking down, and there is an evident restlessness. Certain kinds of action can still be written there, especially when what is ordinarily an inert and conventional self-consciousness, inherent in recent theatre history, can be actively used, as in some of Brecht, as an experience rather than a method: an awareness of presence, challenge, alternative ways of seeing, participation, breaking the line between audience and stage.

But it is in a different direction from that of the majority forms, in cinema and television. There the drama can move beyond representation and mime, to direct production. For the enclosed sensibility, this is a loss of the meaning of theatre. For the newly open and mobile experience, it is an unparalleled opportunity, and the dramatist can, in new ways, write his action directly. Live performance, of course, is given up, and this is some loss, especially in terms of existing kinds of performance. But what is gained is the possibility of control, in the essential continuity of creation and production. A dramatic action can be composed, in its final form, in a way much more satisfactory than the apparent finality of print, which, as we have seen, turns out, in performance, to need radical reworking to become drama, unless, as in certain situations in the past, the conventions are so settled that the creation and the performance can be essentially written in a single text. Those settled conditions are unlikely to recur; they belonged with particular and now unavailable societies; only permanent companies, in this place and that, can offer, locally, any comparable integrity.

A dramatic action can then be composed, in its final form, by the use of the camera, in television and film. But in practice this is still very difficult, because of the transfer of habits from the theatres, and because of the quite new problems of writing which the dramatist encounters. To write an action, for this means of performance, is not simply to write a report of an action, or even its detailed description; it is also to write the movements as they are to be made, and simultaneously the ways in which the movements are to be seen. To write a 'scene', again, is not to write a general description, and of course not one or two static settings, but to integrate all that is to be seen with the primary writing of movements and viewpoints. What had been separated, as actors' movements and settings, must now be written in a single form. Speech, similarly, and any associated sound, must be written within this form, and yet, in another way, must contain this form: not words in front of a background, nor words accompanying movement, but words, scene and movement in a single dimension of writing.

The difficulties are enormous. As Bergman noted, some of the essential notation does not yet exist. And it is then possible for writers to retreat to 'the story which others adapt for performance', or for the writer-director, more often in practice the director-writer, to emerge as the dominant figure. The writer who is not a technician can then run for the theatres, and leave the new forms alone. The major expense of this kind of production, and the commercial or bureaucratic pressures which can bear so heavily, have already made an atmosphere from which many people involved have wanted to run.

The opportunities, however, remain. Not only in methods, but in the existence of audiences, not simply larger but of a different kind: untrained to existing theatrical conventions, and sometimes surprisingly open to new dramatic experience: to new relations, in fact, between dramatists and audiences, of a more open and public kind. Some of the essential writing has to be done in forms moving away from print: in writing and recording voices – not only local rhythms but more general rhythms and sequences – and in stills and in actual work at the place of production. This co-operative work has to be consciously learned by a writer. It is often avoided because of the fear of 'creation by committee', but it need not be always like this, and in some actual cases has not been like it. In a slowly and consciously assembled form, very similar in that respect to writing, co-operation can be very different from what is possible in a relatively sudden and separate performance. In these conditions the new methods can in practice be made.

## CONCLUSION

I have taken the argument this far, from account and classification to criticism and recommendation, because a serious interest in drama in performance must always, in the end, move to what is now actually happening. The practical details belong to specific work: not methods but experiences: actual texts in performance. What begins, though, as a practical problem in writing needs to go, sometimes, into history and theory: as a way of clearing the mind and of beginning a discussion.

What I hope this essay has done, in its several practical examples of plays in performance, and then in argument, is to show, by the facts of variation, not only the rigidity of existing orthodox formulas, but also the openings, the possibilities, and of course the restraints, in the existing situation. For any dramatic writer, the problem of the relation between text and performance is what he takes, repeatedly, to his table; what he has been taking, in such differing circumstances, for more than two thousand years. For any actor, designer and director, the same kind of problem – of moving the writing through to an actual production – is permanent, though in its very permanence, as for the writer, various, experimental, changing. And for readers and audiences, these varying activities and relations, though they may not directly work on them, are there all the time, so that what happens between text and performance is a continuing concern, in all that major area of writing and acting that is our traditional and our living drama.

# Select List of Books for Reference and Further Reading

A. Pickard-Cambridge, *The Theatre of Dionysus at Athens*. Oxford: The Clarendon Press, 1956.

A. Pickard-Cambridge, *The Dramatic Festivals at Athens*. Oxford: The Clarendon Press, 1953.

A. Pickard-Cambridge, *Dithyramb, Tragedy and Comedy*. Oxford: The Clarendon Press, 1927.

R. C. Flickinger, *The Greek Theatre and its Drama*, 4th ed. Chicago: University of Chicago Press, 1936.

D. Grene and R. Lattimore, *Greek Tragedies*, Vol. 1. Chicago: Phoenix Books, University of Chicago Press, 1960.

H. D. F. Kitto, *Form and Meaning in Drama. A Study of Six Greek Plays and of Hamlet*. London: Methuen, 1956.

E. K. Chambers, *The Medieval Stage*, 2 Vols. Oxford: O.U.P., 1903.

E. Norris, *The Ancient Cornish Drama*, 2 vols. Oxford: O.U.P., 1859.

K. Young, *The Drama of the Medieval Church*. Oxford: the Clarendon Press, 1933.

R. Southern, *The Medieval Theatre in the Round*. London: Faber & Faber, 1957.

V. A. Kolve, *The Play Called Corpus Christi*. London: Edward Arnold, 1966.

O. B. Hardison, Jr., *Christian Rite and Christian Drama in the Middle Ages*. Baltimore, Md: Johns Hopkins Press, 1965.

G. Wickham, *Early English Stages*, 2 vols. London: Routledge & Kegan Paul, 1959, 1963.

A. W. Pollard, *Everyman, with other Interludes, including Eight Miracle Plays*, 8th edition. Oxford: the Clarendon Press, 1927.

E. K. Chambers, *The Elizabethan Stage*, 4 vols. Oxford: O.U.P., 1923.

M. C. Bradbrook, *Elizabethan Stage Conditions*. Cambridge: C.U.P., 1932.

M. C. Bradbrook, *Themes and Conventions in Elizabethan Tragedy*. Cambridge: C.U.P., 1935.

M. C. Bradbrook, *The Rise of the Common Player*. London: Chatto & Windus, 1962.

M. C. Bradbrook, *English Dramatic Form*. London: Chatto & Windus, 1965.

W. J. Lawrence, *The Elizabethan Playhouse*, first and second series. Stratford-on-Avon, 1912, 1913.

W. J. Lawrence, *Pre-Restoration Stage Studies*. Cambridge, U.S.A., 1927.

W. J. Lawrence, *The Physical Conditions of the English Public Playhouse*. Cambridge, U.S.A., 1927.

J. C. Adams, *The Globe Playhouse – its design and equipment*. Harvard: Harvard U.P., 1942.

A. Harbage, *Shakespeare's Audience*. New York: Columbia, 1941.

E. W. Naylor, *Shakespeare and Music*, revised edition. London: Dent, 1931.

B. L. Joseph, *Elizabethan Acting*. Oxford: The Clarendon Press, 1951.

A. M. Nagler, *Shakespeare's Stage*. New Haven and London: Yale University Press, 1958.

J. Dover Wilson (ed.) *Antony and Cleopatra*. Cambridge: C.U.P., 1950.

J. R. Brown, *Shakespeare's Plays in Performance*. London: Edward Arnold, 1966.

H. Granville Barker, *Prefaces to Shakespeare*, 2 vols. London: Batsford, 1958.

L. C. Knights, *Some Shakespearean Themes*. London: Chatto & Windus, 1959.

G. Wilson Knight, *The Imperial Theme*. Oxford: the Clarendon Press, 1932.

A. Nicoll, *The English Theatre*. London: Thomas Nelson, 1936.

A. Nicoll, *A History of Restoration Drama 1660–1700*. Cambridge: C.U.P., 1940.

A. Nicoll, *A History of Early Eighteenth Century Drama 1700–1750*. Cambridge: C.U.P., 1929.

## Select List of Books

A. Nicoll, *A History of English Drama – Late Nineteenth Century Drama*. Cambridge: C.U.P., 1959.

G. Rowell, *The Victorian Theatre*. London: O.U.P., 1956.

G. H. Nettleton and A. E. Case (eds.), *British Dramatists from Dryden to Sheridan*. London: Harrap, 1939.

T. W. Robertson, *Caste (with Stage Business)*. New York: Robert M. De Witt, (n.d.? 1867).

J. Northam, *Ibsen's Dramatic Method*. London: Faber & Faber, 1953.

P. F. D. Tennant, *Ibsen's Dramatic Technique*. Cambridge: Bowes & Bowes, 1948.

K. Stanislavsky, *An Actor Prepares*. London: Bles, 1936.

*The Seagull Produced by Stanislavsky*, text and score. London: Dennis Dobson, 1952.

D. Magarshack, *Stanislavsky on the Art of the Stage*. London: Faber & Faber, 1950.

T. S. Eliot, *Poetry and Drama*. London: Faber & Faber, 1951.

D. I. Vesey (transl.) *The Life of Galileo*, in *Bertolt Brecht: Plays*, vol. 1. London: Methuen, 1960.

R. Gray, *Brecht*, in the series Writers and Critics. London and Edinburgh: Oliver & Boyd, 1961.

N. Marshall, *The Other Theatre*. London: John Lehmann, 1947.

J. Willett (transl.) *Brecht on the Art of Theatre*. London: Methuen, 1964.

I. Bergman, *Four Screenplays*. London: Secker & Warburg, 1960.

V. I. Pudovkin, *Film Acting*. London: George Newnes, 1935.

M. Redgrave, *The Actor's Ways and Means*. London: Heinemann, 1953.

M. Orrom, *Film and its Dramatic Techniques* (in *Preface to Film* by M. Orrom and R. Williams). London: Film Drama Ltd., 1954.

W. Archer, *The Old Drama and the New*. New York: Dodd, Mead & Co., 1926.

W. B. Yeats, *Essays and Introductions*. London: Macmillan, 1961.

R. Peacock, *The Poet in the Theatre*. London: Macgibbon & Kee, 1961.

R. Peacock, *The Art of Drama*. London: Routledge & Kegan Paul, 1957.

U. Ellis-Fermor, *The Frontiers of Drama*. London: Methuen, 1964.

J. L. Styan, *Elements of Drama*. Cambridge: C.U.P., 1960.

E. Gordon Craig, *On the Art of the Theatre*. London: Heinemann, 1911.

E. Bentley, *The Playwright as Thinker*. New York: Meridian, 1955.

F. Fergusson, *The Idea of a Theatre*. Princeton University Press, U.S.A., 1949.

P. D. Hazard (ed.), *T.V. as Art*. Illinois, U.S.A.: National Council of Teachers of English, 1964.

L. Kitchin, *Mid-Century Drama*. London: Faber & Faber, 1962.

# Index

# MORE ABOUT PENGUINS
## AND PELICANS

*Penguinews*, which appears every month, contains details of all the new books issued by Penguins as they are published. From time to time it is supplemented by *Penguins in Print*, which is a complete list of all available books published by Penguins. (There are well over three thousand of these.)

A specimen copy of *Penguinews* will be sent to you free on request, and you can become a subscriber for the price of the postage. For a year's issues (including the complete lists) please send 30p if you live in the United Kingdom, or 60p if you live elsewhere. Just write to Dept EP, Penguin Books Ltd, Harmondsworth, Middlesex, enclosing a cheque or postal order, and your name will be added to the mailing list.

Note: *Penguinews* and *Penguins in Print* are not available in the U.S.A. or Canada

# THE THEORY OF
# THE MODERN STAGE

An Introduction to Modern Theatre and Drama

*Eric Bentley*

A new anthology, edited by America's leading dramatic critic, in which Artaud, Brecht, Gordon Craig, Stanislavski, and other great theatrical theorists reveal the ideas underlying their productions and point to the possibilities of the modern theatre.

# COMMUNICATIONS

*Raymond Williams*

### REVISED EDITION

Along with *Culture and Society 1780–1950* and *The Long Revolution*, *Communications* has been an influential factor, since it first came out as a Penguin Special, in opening up the new field of cultural studies. It is now re-issued as a Pelican in a revised edition, with more recent statistics and two new appendices.

Raymond Williams contends that society cannot be fully understood without according as much importance to the massive ganglia of communication which link, influence, and shape modern society – newspapers, television, magazines, and radio – as to politics and economics.

This book analyses the contents and methods of these media in detail, noting the influence exercised on them by advertising, and then discusses the controversies surrounding 'high and low culture', 'violence and values' and similar topics.

The author concludes with a full statement of the educational and social reforms needed to provide a 'permanent education' on democratic lines.

Also available (*Not for sale in the U.S.A.*)

CULTURE AND SOCIETY 1780–1950
THE LONG REVOLUTION